THE ADVENTURES OF A QUIET SOUL

A Scrapbook of Memories

V. OWEN

ACKNOWLEDGMENTS AND CREDITS

Appreciation is expressed to the following individuals and/or organizations for sharing ideas, suggestions, research information, talent, baseball memorabilia, and counsel for this book.

- Dave Anderson, New York,
- Bettman Archive, New York
- Marty Boland, Santa Clara, CA, Marv's lifelong friend
- Jim Campbell, General Manager, retired, Detroit Tigers
- Detroit Free Press, Detroit, MI
- Detroit News, Detroit, MI
- Detroit Tiger Fans, Detroit, MI
- Detroit Tiger Organization, Detroit, MI
- Tina Dinsmore, Santa Cruz, CA, super secretary
- Dick Dobbins, Alamo, CA
- Lyn Dremalas, Palo Alto, CA, friend
- Former President Gerald R. Ford, Rancho Mirage, CA
- Mrs. Charles L. Gehringer, MI
- Bill Geoffroy, Tucson, AZ, writer
- Mrs. Geo. Geoffroy, CA, Marv's sister
- Steve Gietschier, The Sporting News
- Terry Grand, Los Gatos, CA, photographer
- Mardie Gregg, PA, reader
- Kathy Guinn, MD, reader
- Ross Hamilton, WA, photographer
- Ernie Harwell, Detroit, MI, retired announcer
- Chuck Hildebrand, CA, writer
- Larry Jinks, former publisher San Jose Mercury News
- Jim Jennings, Santa Clara, CA, Marv's lifelong friend
- Mr. & Mrs. Elmer Kapp, MI, super fans
- Dennis Kapp, Detroit, MI, Universal Design
- Patricia Kelly, National Baseball Library and Archive, Cooperstown, NY
- Bill Kirkland, NC
- K. Kirwan, CA, student
- Herman Krabbenhoft, Schenectady, NY, editor
- Ed La Pere, Taylor, MI, artist
- David P. Mamuscia, MI
- John McHale, Palm City, FL, retired baseball executive

- Bill O'Neal, Carthage, TX
- Robert D. Opie, Santa Clara, CA
- Joan Owen, Marv's daughter-in-law, WA
- Skip Owen, WA, Marv's son
- Dwayne Padon, Lexington, NC, super fan
- David Pietrusza, NY, Pres. SABR
- Herb Quinn, WA, photographer
- Ripley Entertainment, Inc., FL
- Bill Rogell, Newport Richey, FL, retired Tiger shortstop
- Rev. Jerome C. Romanowski, Holy Name Society, Laurel Springs, NJ
- Ron Root, Aptos, CA, teacher, photographer, artist
- San Jose Mercury, San Jose, CA
- Roger Sita, WA
- Alice Sloane, Senior Director, retired, Detroit Tigers, Detroit, MI
- Rick Smith, Gen. Manager, Bakersfield Dodgers, Bakersfield, CA
- John Spalding, San Jose, CA, writer
- Sports Library AA Foundation, LA
- Tad Teranishi, CA
- The Oregonian, Portland, OR
- The Sporting News, St. Louis, MO
- University of Santa Clara, Santa Clara, CA
- Rita Waldorf, CA, super fan
- Virginia Walmer, KS, writer
- William Weiss, statistician, CA
- Wide World Photo, New York, NY
- Mrs. Joseph Yoggerst, CA, Marv's sister

In memory of Mother, Father, Evie, John, and Lu

IN APPRECIATION

Marv lived for baseball and was touched by different influences throughout his career. He never forgot those who influenced him the most:

- his mother and father who gave him complete support throughout their lives,
- Babe Ruth whom he first saw in San Jose in 1928 when the Babe and Lou Gehrig played in an exhibition game,
- Jack Graham of the San Jose Mercury whom Marv credited with giving him the greatest professional boost,
- "Happy" Luke Williams who selected Marv as the regular first sacker for the Consolidated Laundry team in the 1920s and hired him as a laundry route driver on Saturdays,
- Father J. H. Donahue, S.J., who was an influence from the time he and Marv first met at Bellarmine College Preparatory until Father Donohue's death in 1972,
- Buddy Leitch, sports editor and columnist for the San Jose News, who, similar to Jack Graham, gave great sports coverage to Marv,
- Coach Justin Fitzgerald, (Fitz) the coach at Santa Clara who recognized the potential of his star first baseman and who guided him into a professional baseball career,
- Scouts or baseball personnel who showed interest in Marv in the late 1920s as a professional prospect: Ira F. Thomas, Connie Mack, Roy T. Mack*, C. C. Slapnicka; and Bill Klepper, who signed him for his first professional baseball contract in 1930 with the Seattle Club of the Pacific Coast League. It was later in the 1940s that Bill Klepper and Marv joined forces again, Bill as business manager of the Portland Beavers of the Pacific Coast League and Marv the Beavers' player and then player/manager. In Portland, Marv's team won the pennant in 1945.

- Charlie Gehringer, Detroit Tigers, 2nd baseman (1924 through 1942) who became a lifelong friend to the rookie Marv Owen. Charlie was best man at Marv's wedding in Detroit in 1938 and Marv was best man at Charlie's wedding in San Jose in 1949.
- John J. McHale who in the 1950s (1951 through 1956) was the Tigers' Assistant Farm Director and Farm Director and then, (in 1957) became the Detroit Tigers General Manager. In 1952 until 1954 Marv managed three Detroit farm clubs: Davenport, Durham and Valdosta. In 1954 Marv moved into the Tiger scouting department. Marv and John (later President of the Montreal Expos) kept in touch and corresponded for over 40 years.

*One of Connie Mack's sons.

"I feel fortunate that I've worked with so many great people in baseball and met so many nice people including all the hundreds of baseball fans."

— M. O.

HOW THE BOOK CAME TO BE

In the late 1980's when my brother Marv and I were going through his baseball stuff, he would sometimes reminisce. Often, he enjoyed telling me baseball stories. Then one day I asked him if together we could write a baseball book. We decided first he would see what he could find in his old newspaper clippings and baseball scrapbooks that would bring back memories to him, then he would tell me things that I would write down and lastly, he would give me access to much of his baseball memorabilia. As a hobby, he had written poems about anything of interest to him at the moment. There are binders filled with these rhymes, so they, too, are part of the book. Whenever you see M.O. by one of the poems, you know it is one of Marv's. Other sources of information came from oldtimers of his era, old movie film footage, faded newspaper clippings, correspondence, and videotapes.

Marv (John to his four sisters) was always my big brother. He let me try out his bike when I was six and he was nineteen. He invited me to ride with him occasionally on Saturdays in the laundry truck to Gilroy as once a week he drove his Consolidated Laundry route. On some Sundays, we would walk through San Jose State campus from our home on South Sixth Street in San Jose to downtown St. Joseph's Church. When he began playing with the Tigers in Detroit he sent me letters, often including a dollar bill or maybe a five. In the early Thirties when he was a Detroit Tiger and living at the Wolverine Hotel (or the Wolf House, as the players living there called it), he invited my mother, father and me to stay as his guests at the hotel so we could see him and the Tigers play at home. I was 14. When I graduated from high school in 1937 he gave me my first gold wristwatch.

He was always my big brother.

On June 22, 1991 John died at the age of 85. We hadn't written the book, but we had gathered a lot of material about earlier baseball times, especially the 1930's. Before he died, John settled on the title "The Thrill of It All" as the right one for our book*. He felt that title expressed exactly what his baseball career meant to him.

If he were here to read this book today, he'd probably call it his fathead book.

---

* Some earlier writer had used that title, so we didn't use it.

His name is Marvin.
Last name is Owen.
About self does little blowin'.
Middle name is James.
Leo is his confirmation name.
Baseball is his game.

— Marv Owen.

Saturday

Dear Babe:(Vi)

Early this morning, I do not know what the hour was-but my brain was "a-workin"-as it came up with many ideas about things that happened during my career (and my time in baseball)-but I did not have a pad next to my bed, but will from now on have a pad on the bureau next to me-so when these ideas hit me, I will turn on the light and jot em down. But later today when I finally got out of bed at 7:25 (late for me) I went to my pad and wrote down many of em that I had in my mind earlier in the morning-but I did not get all of em-as memory failed me-so I won't let that happen again. Believe a page could be written (or maybe more) on Gerry Walker as a player and the crazy antics he would do on the field.

I think we (you and I) will have trouble having enough for a small book but I will start working on my notes-and from now on, whenever a "book idea" hits me, I will jot it down-in fact. believe I will also have a pad in the car in case a thought hits me while I am driving.

(Marv)

(Photo credit: Herb Quinn, Wa)

Awards, Honors, Records, Events

Marv was reticent about bringing attention to himself. He was thrilled to be a part of major league baseball and grateful and honest about his skills. Sorting through the memorabilia he saved, these were some of the recorded events:

1906 Marvin James Owen was born March 22 at the family home at Bassett and Beech St., Agnew, California;

1906 On April 18 the great earthquake and fire devastated San Francisco, 41 miles north of Agnew. Marv was less than a month old.;

1919 Owen family moved to San Jose, California;

1926 Received a scholarship to Santa Clara College;

1928 Saw Babe Ruth and Lou Gehrig play an exhibition game in San Jose;

1930 Elected captain of Santa Clara College (later Santa Clara University) varsity baseball team;

1930 Appointed baseball coach at Santa Clara College;

1930 Graduated from Santa Clara College in May;

1930 Signed with Seattle of the Pacific Coast League, was switched from playing 1st base (his collegiate position) to 3rd base. In four successive days, his first in professional baseball, he played four different infield positions: first, second, third and shortstop;

1931 Began his career with the Detroit Tigers;

1931 Hit his first major league home run May 7;

1932 Hit a home run in the 9th inning to give Newark the International League's Little World Series Championship in October;

1932 Was voted the most valuable player in the International League;

1934 Began a triple play with Hank Greenberg against the Cleveland Indians at Briggs Stadium;

1934 Led the American League third basemen in RBI;

1934 Led the American League third basemen in putouts: 202;

1934 Didn't miss a game playing with Detroit Tigers (154);

1934 Had the most unassisted double plays, 2 (for third basemen) in two consecutive games, April 28 and 29;

1934 Was nominated for MVP award in American League;

1934 Participated in Detroit Tigers World Series, first pennant winning team of Tigers in 25 years;

1934 Engaged in Owen-Medwick incident in World Series. Baseball Commissioner Judge Landis, in order to restore order, told Medwick to leave after fans disrupted the game by throwing fruit and debris at Medwick on the field;

1934 Was a member of the greatest RBI Infield: 1st base Hank Greenberg (.339 batting average and 139 RBI); 2nd base Charley Gehringer (.356 batting average and 127 RBI); shortstop Billy Rogell (.296 batting average and 100 RBI); 3rd base Marv Owen (.317 batting average and 96 RBI);

1934 Appointed honorary Santa Clara County Deputy Sheriff No. A1;

1934 Received The Sporting News Award and Trophy;

1935 Played in World Series: Tigers vs the Cubs; Tigers won;

1935 Switched from third to first base in the World Series when regular first sacker Hank Greenberg was injured;

1935 Had 4 assists at 1st base in one game of World Series (October), a record for that time. Was equaled by Don Mincher in October 1965;

1935 Tied the American League record of 9 assists at 3rd base;

1935 Holds the World Series (2) record with 31 consecutive hitless times at bat;

1935 Hit a single in the final game of the World Series which tied the game and enabled the Tigers to win the game and the series in the 9th inning;

1935 Had a clutch hitting index (CHI) of 139; in 1936 had 137. Over 100 is superior. Joe Cronin once called him the toughest No. 7 hitter in the league.

1936 Didn't miss a game while playing with Detroit (154);

1936 Had over 100 RBI along with Simmons, Goslin and Gehringer;

1936 Led the American League third basemen in RBI;

1937 Had an American League leading 3rd base Fielding Average of .970, 106 games, 10 errors;

1937 Was a member of the Detroit Tiger team that scored 20 runs on August 14; 20-7 against the St. Louis Browns;

1938 Married Detroit teacher Violet Walsh. Charlie Gehringer was best man.

1939 On June 12 participated in Baseball Centennial Celebration at Cooperstown, New York as one of the representatives of the Chicago White Sox;

1939 Hit four doubles April 23, in one game, to tie the record;

1940 After 9 seasons in the major leagues, had more walks (338) then strikeouts (283);

1941 Named by Walter O. Briggs, former owner of the Detroit Tigers, as 3rd baseman for his all-time Detroit Tigers Squad;

1941 Had highest 3rd base fielding average in Pacific Coast League (with Portland Beavers), .954 in 140 games;

1941 Selected as Northern California All Star Team Member;

1944 Became Player/Manager for Portland Beavers, Pacific Coast League;

1945 Held the highest fielding average in the history of the Pacific Coast League at that time: .986 and batting average of .311;

1945 Managed Portland Beavers to Pacific Coast League pennant;

1945 Became the father of Marvin Owen II (Skip);

1947 Named Champion of Champions in Santa Clara County, California;

1949 Was Best Man at Charlie Gehringer's wedding to Josephine Stillen in San Jose, California;

1954 Became a Detroit Tiger scout;

1958 Participated in Detroit Old Timers celebration at Briggs Stadium; also participating were Ty Cobb, Sam Crawford, Charlie Gehringer, Mickey Cochrane and Hank Greenberg, all Hall of Fame Tigers;

1958 Designed and supervised construction of "The Trap" a 9 foot wall to sharpen fielding skills of the infielders at Tigertown, Lakeland, Florida;

1959 Participated in Lakeland, Florida's 1934-59 Twenty-fifth Anniversary of Detroit's participation in '34 World Series. Received key to city;

1962 Honored as one of 15 Santa Clara University All-Time Athletic Stars;

1968 Named to Sportswriters, Broadcasters Santa Clara Valley Sports Hall of Fame at Banquet of Champions;

1972 Named to Bellarmine High School (California) Athletic Hall of Fame;

1978 Answered request of National Baseball Hall of Fame and Museum at Cooperstown, New York to donate his professional baseball glove which was used to hold seven regulation big league baseballs in his hand;

1983 Participated in retirement of Greenberg's #5 and Gehringer's #2 at Greenberg-Gehringer Day;

1988 Donated complete 1934 Detroit Tigers World Series baseball uniform to Domino's Pizza Foundation for the Detroit Tigers Archives and Museum (the uniform is now at the Corporate Archives at Little Caesar's World Headquarters).

1991 Died in Mountain View, CA., June 22.

TABLE OF CONTENTS

I. GROWING UP

Agnew Depot
Agnew, California

GROWING UP IN THE COUNTRY

Agnew, California, 41 miles south of San Francisco, in the early 1900's was a tiny country town with a train station, a grammar school, a garage, a coffee shop, a state hospital, and a post office. In 1910 the Santa Clara County directory had 174 names listed as the population of Agnew. The surrounding land was primarily pear orchards, agricultural crops and dairy farms. Open fields were close to all the little homes. The Owen family: father James (born in England), mother Kate (born in Lawrence, Kansas), freckle-faced son Marvin, daughters Evelyn, Lucile and Dorothy lived in a small one story wooden house on the corner of Bassett and Beech Streets across from the railroad station. Grandfather, Smith Nichols, built two houses on their land behind their home. James worked at the state hospital as a switchboard operator and ward attendant; Kate was a homemaker and mother. The four children, all born in California, attended the Agnew grammar school. The school had one room, one teacher, teaching grades 1 through 8 with about fifty students in all. In late summer when the children were not in school, they and their mother sorted pears at the Montague ranch. When Marvin and other boys his age picked pears, they were sometimes scolded for throwing pears instead of working.

Marv was shy but when it came to throwing pears, he wasn't shy and enjoyed the sport! Shyness was with him all his life.

Why Be Shy?

Worst thing in the world is to be shy.
Now I will tell you why.
Shy person is never in front, on stage or in a show
He or she is always sitting in the back row.
Shy person seldom wants any attention
Being that way one misses a lot of fun.
We don't understand how some are born with shyness,
And others are extroverts, out of life they get the best.
We, the shyers don't enjoy being in the limelight.
We prefer by all means to be out of sight.
Extroverts have the world by the tail.
Shyers in front many times fail.
Shyness is always there. With age some might lose it.
It isn't accomplished overnight but bit by bit,
You haven't conquered it yet,
But in time you will, I bet.

M.O.

Marv saved his earnings from picking pears. After many seasons, when he was twelve he had enough money to buy himself a bicycle. On that great day he bought his own bicycle, cycled to Santa Clara (about 5 miles) with his friend, bought them tickets to a movie and afterwards bought them each a chocolate sundae before they cycled home again. All of that was big news to the other kids in the neighborhood. In the late spring and early summer, the whole family picked tomatoes at farms on the outskirts of Santa Clara. The four children snacked on tomatoes when they were hungry, which was the case if they had been to school first and came to work directly after school. Sometimes they and their mother picked new tender mustard leaves from the fields to have for dinner at night.

When the family first lived in Agnew, they had a horse, Babe, and a buggy. They later gave Babe to Grandfather Nichols. The family's first automobiles were Chevrolets.

In the open fields of Agnew, Marv began his training for a life of baseball. He threw rocks at passing freight trains; he threw rocks at almost anything that moved.

*Marv and the new bike
January 1919*

3

You can roll a ball.
You can hit a ball.
You can throw a ball.
You can shoot a ball.
You can punt a ball.
You can serve a ball.
You can kick a ball
You can drop a ball.
You can tee-off a ball.
You can bat a ball.
You can sling a ball.
You can miss a ball.
You can pitch a ball.
You can underhand a ball.
You can toss a ball.
You can spin a ball.
You can curve a ball.

M.O.

Agnew School, 1918
Agnew, California
Marv is last one in front in lower right. Marv's sister Lucile is in the 3rd row, the first girl on the right.

4

When he was between eight and twelve, he and his dad played catch and hit fungoes religiously. James was a regular on the Agnew State Hospital baseball team, so his son learned from seeing his dad and his dad's team play ball. James was a good father and a patient teacher when he taught his son the skills of baseball. The only baseball for kids in the neighborhood was playing "pick-up team" or "one-a-cat." There were no organized leagues for ten, eleven or twelve year olds in Agnew. Marv learned his baseball skills primarily from his father and practiced those skills with him even into his professional career.

Fifteen years later in an interview during a summer visit to Detroit, Mrs. James E. Owen, Marv's mother had this to say. "Marvin's father was a baseball player, you know, and consequently I followed the game very closely. Then when Marvin became interested in the sport, which was practically from the time he was able to toddle around and throw a ball, we did all we could to encourage him. We recognized early that Marvin had tremendous natural ability, and there never was any question but that baseball would be his chosen career. My only objection to his stepping into professional company sooner than he did was that I insisted he acquire a college education first. Otherwise he would have started several years earlier than 1930, when he joined Seattle."

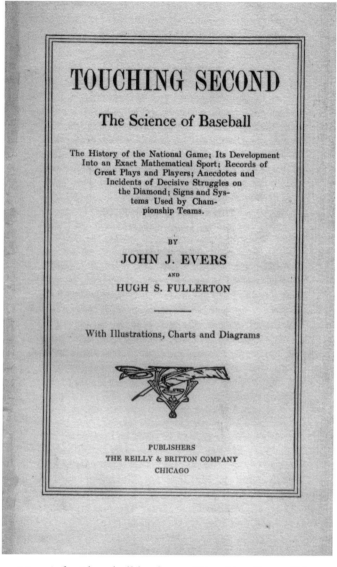

TOUCHING SECOND

The Science of Baseball

The History of the National Game; Its Development Into an Exact Mathematical Sport; Records of Great Plays and Players; Anecdotes and Incidents of Decisive Struggles on the Diamond; Signs and Systems Used by Championship Teams.

BY

JOHN J. EVERS

AND

HUGH S. FULLERTON

With Illustrations, Charts and Diagrams

PUBLISHERS
THE REILLY & BRITTON COMPANY
CHICAGO

James Owen, first in bottom row on left
Agnew State Hospital Baseball Team

Marv's first baseball book was "Touching Second" by Evers and Fullerton. It was printed in 1910 and Marv probably purchased it in a second hand store about 1920. He saved it even though it was well worn.

5

When Marv was thirteen, he and his family left Agnew and the country to move to the city of San Jose. This meant changing schools, saying goodbye to friends like the Hughes and the Ligouris, leaving the open mustard fields and going to a large city. Everything comfortable and well known was in Agnew; San Jose meant the unknown. Moving was tough for a shy kid.

Bob, the family pet, was never fenced in or tied in the yard. After a warning, he was picked up by animal control and destroyed. The whole family was heartbroken.

The picture shows from left to right: Marvin (standing), Mother Kate, Dorothy, Lucile, James (standing) and Bob, the dog.

I was never much of a fisherman
Too much wasted time in fishing
I want more action!
Fishing was never included at anytime in my wishes
Never had any desire to catch different kinds of fishes.
My dad was never interested in fishing, though,
As a youngster he used to take me hunting, I know.
I'd walk in front of him and he'd give me hell
"Get behind me, Marv" he would shout and yell.
He would hunt all kinds of birds
Robins, Meadow Larks, Kildeer and Quail.
They were all so pretty I was glad when he did fail.
But my dad was an excellent shot,
And every bird he aimed at, he got.

M.O.

When the family first moved to San Jose, they rented a house on East San Salvador St. near San Jose Normal College until they were able to purchase a home. They had lived very frugally in Agnew and had few expenses. Marv's dad had inherited his mother's San Jose property on Maple St. in 1913, so with that and the rental income from the Agnew houses, the family was able, with a very low down payment, to buy a large duplex on South Sixth Street in San Jose that was the family home for over 50 years.

Even in the years just before and during the Great Depression no one in the family suffered severe hardships. The children did know that Mother and Father would often let tenants be late with the rent or skip a month in certain special occasions, and they knew, too, that Mother always gave a hot meal to any beggar who came to the back door. She had begun feeding hoboes in Agnew when they would come from the freight trains at the train station across the street.

In order to make ends meet, both parents would often figure out ways to trade or barter services for needed items. For instance, a renter, who was a painter, might paint the house for free rent.

A monthly charge account was kept at the small corner grocery store, so that the food bill only came once a month. After a few years they were able to purchase the small store and their grocery bill was subtracted from the storekeeper's rent.

These were the only instances that the brother and sisters knew about money being tight. In comparison with people in the eastern and middle western United States suffering from the depression, the Owen Family was well to do: they had a house, a car, clothes and food, and paid their bills.

Moving into San Jose

Was 13 years old when moved
from country to town
At that time really in the country
enjoyed walking around.
In those young days was a good walker
But then as now not much of a talker.

When folks decided to move to San Jose
I did not want to go that way.
Didn't want to move in summer, spring,
winter or fall,
I preferred to remain out in the country
and that's all.
When the movers were moving us to San Jose,
It was in the country I just wanted to stay.

M.O.

Once settled in San Jose, Marv and two of his sisters, Lucile and Dorothy were enrolled at Lowell School at 7th and Reed Streets, the neighborhood grammar school. The small one room Agnew school of forty or more pupils they had left behind, did not compare to the new school. Lowell School by comparison was huge; it had about 700 boys and girls, many teachers and it was two stories high with lots of rooms. Third grader Dorothy was so terrified, her older sister Lucile had to stay with her on the playground to comfort her. Dorothy's teeth chattered every morning before school for a full week.

Marv, though still shy, found consolation in the fact that a baseball field, Reed Field, was close by the school; this was definitely to his liking. The Reed name is historically important to San Jose. James Frazier Reed was an early Donner Party organizer who came to California. Some of the San Jose streets, Reed, Margaret, Martha, Virginia and Keyes, were named after the Reed family.

In addition to moving into a new home in San Jose, a new member of the family was born. Marv had three sisters already, so it was expected that the new baby would be a little brother, Leo; but it wasn't that way at all. A baby girl, Viola (Babe), joined the family. So now there were four girls and one boy, seven family members.

The first baseball team with real uniforms that Marv joined was the San Jose High School team. His friends Ray Dwyer and Howard "Lefty" Blethen were on that team along with exactly six other players. The complete roster was nine players. Or maybe they only had nine uniforms and had to limit the number of players. Many years later, Ray became the manager of the Resetar Hotel in Watsonville, California, and

Typing Medal for
Speed and Accuracy

"Lefty" became a school administrator in California.

The first time Ray Dwyer and Marv, two fair-skinned, freckled-faced kids, met at Reed Field they each nicknamed the other "Freck." The nickname did not stay with Ray, but it did stay with Marv throughout his career. Another pal at Reed Field was Art Hunt who later joined the Pacific Coast League. When he retired in 1939, he joined the Washington State Patrol as a trooper.

Marv transferred to the Jesuit Bellarmine College Prep School as a "day dog" (as opposed to a boarding student) and joined the baseball team. In high school, Marty Boland, a good friend, became a fellow "day dog" and played on the baseball team. Marty and Marv were both excellent typists as well as good athletes. In high school Marv received a special typing medal for speed and accuracy. The San Jose Mercury Herald, the local newspaper, with Jack Graham, sports writer, covered the Bellarmine games. After the games, Marv and Marty would hurry to type out the game results and go down to Lightstone Alley to turn in to the night press foreman what had been typed. Because their reports were typed, their games by far got the best coverage. Marv always said the person who gave him the greatest boost initially in his career was San Jose Mercury Herald sports writer, Jack Graham. One story that Marty tells is about the time he was asked to include the other team's three substitutes (whose names he didn't know) so he typed Nina, Pinta, Santa Maria and that was what appeared in the lineup in the paper the next day. Whatever they turned in was printed.

9

Reed Field-early 1920's

The well known "good old days" away back when—"Freck" Owen was playing for Lowell grammar school and the sandlotting Dodgers of 1922, a club that sent more than one youngster into faster company. Remember them?
Back row, left to right—
Les Sheridan, St Mary's, 1b. and lf.;
Stanley Adams, Hawthorne, p,;
Marvin Owen, Lowell, ss and 1b.;
Ralph Johnson, St. Mary's, 2b.;
Duke Penniman, Lowell, utility.
Center row—
Howard "Lefty" Blethen, Lowell, 1b.;
Bud Raley. Lowell, rf.;
Art Hunt, Lowell, cf.;
Emmett "Red" Sheridan, St. Mary's c.
Front row—
Ray Dwyer, Lowell, 3b.;
Bud Crowley, St. Mary's, mascot.

Reed Field
San Jose, CA, 1923
Top left is Marv Owen; bottom left is Howard "Lefty" Blethen; bottom right next to last is Ray Dwyer.

What was San Jose/Santa Clara like? In the late 1920's and in the 1930's San Jose was often called the "Garden City" and Santa Clara Valley was the "Valley of Hearts' Delight." The natural beauty of the area was highlighted once a year by the Fiesta de las Rosas where flower-filled floats, beautiful fiesta queens and attendants would be on parade. Shade trees and gardens added to the attractiveness of the area. The Alameda was a tree-lined avenue with expensive homes. The campus at San Jose State College was filled with multiple kinds of trees, rolling lawns over much open space. Streetcars were an important mode of transportation from the outskirts of San Jose and Santa Clara. Students going to College of Santa Clara, Bellarmine, Notre Dame and San Jose Normal often used the streetcars. Bellarmine Prep School was on the site of the original College of the Pacific; that neighborhood was called College Park. San Jose was an example of a medium sized western town with much to offer.

A float from the Fiesta de las Roses Parade

What were the sights and smells around San Jose in the '20s and '30s?*

▶ The peanut wagons at First and Santa Clara and at First Street near William,

▶ Chatterton Bakery on South 2nd Street with fresh, yeasty, bread smells,

▶ Tamales at Stokes Tamale Parlor on North First Street near the Victory Theatre,

▶ Elm leaves in the compost pits on the San Jose State campus along San Carlos Street,

▶ Cigar smells from Crystal Billiards on San Fernando Street,

▶ Across the street, Rampone's Delicatessen that smelled like French bread, raviolis and olive oil,

▶ The sweet, heavy smell from the San Jose Creamery on South First Street,

▶ Mustard greens picked for dinner from the fields early in the season before the leaves got tough and the plants went to seed,

▶ The dry, summer smell of Alum Rock park — a mixture of oak trees, sulphur, mineral water and dust,

▶ Wendt's Meat Market at North Market Street,

▶ Potato chips at Eggo on Julian Street,

▶ Apples at the Ogier Ranch on Montague Road,

▶ Sawdust and floor oil in classrooms at San Jose High at Seventh and San Fernando,

▶ The same smell at the Morris Dailey Auditorium at San Jose State,

▶ The fruit smells from Barron and Gray Can Company at the peak of the canning season in summer vacation,

*Some of these descriptions were sent by the author to Wally Trabing and appeared in his column in the Santa Cruz Sentinel, May 9, 1982.

on South Second Street,

- ▶ A sad smell from the Santa Clara Tannery,
- ▶ The chlorine at the Y.W.C.A. indoor swimming pool on South Second Street,
- ▶ The burning sulphur fumes to protect apricots on the trays in the dry yards at Rosenberg's in Santa Clara,
- ▶ The Warburton's enchiladas on Alviso Street in Santa Clara,
- ▶ Danish pastry and chocolates at O'Brien's Candy Store on South First Street,
- ▶ Willson's (two ll's) Cafeteria on San Antonio Street,
- ▶ The Oyster Loaf on Santa Clara Street,
- ▶ The Alameda French Bakery on Pleasant Street,
- ▶ Grass and clover and daisies being mowed on campus at San Jose State when it seemed there was more land in lawns than in buildings,
- ▶ Bartlett pears from the Montague Ranch Riverside Farm on Montague Road,
- ▶ The Esperanza Dairy on The Agnew – Alviso Road,
- ▶ Reject pears from the canneries as the fruit floated in the salt water at Alviso,
- ▶ Babe Arzino's Fish Market on North Market Street,
- ▶ Exotic smells from the Genovesi Central Grocery across from the St. Claire Hotel on Market Street,
- ▶ Tomato smells at U.S. Products Cannery,
- ▶ The heady smell of apricot and cherry blossoms throughout the valley in springtime,
- ▶ Roses from the floats of the Fiesta de las Rosas on display on San Carlos Street,

- ▶ Halla's Coffee Co. on South Second Street,
- ▶ Cookie smells from Wilson's Bakery in Santa Clara,
- ▶ The inviting smell from the Beechnut Candy Co. down past St. Mary's School,
- ▶ The Crystal Creamery on Santa Clara Street,
- ▶ The basement of the old Italian Hotel on San Augustine - soup, raviolis, chicken, spaghetti to take home,
- ▶ The smell of trains at the First and Bassett S.P. Depot,
- ▶ The sweet smell of prunes (not plums!) drying on the drying trays in summer.

Another float at So. 7th and San Carlos Sts., San Jose

High school and college baseball led to other baseball opportunities. When the school team was not scheduled for a game on the weekend, often Marv and others played for the Consolidated Laundry, Garden City Billiards, Knights of Columbus, or San Mateo Blues to name a few. When Marv was about 17, he began playing for Garden City Billiards for Frank Boitano. When he was playing for the Consolidated Laundry, "Happy" Luke Williams, the manager, offered him a Saturday job to drive the Consolidated Laundry truck on the Gilroy route. Sometimes, Marv would invite one of his sisters to enjoy the ride with him.

The baseball games were played at Graham Field, Reed Field, Backesto Park and Sodality Park in San Jose, at College Park in Santa Clara and at City Park in San Mateo. The baseball parks, though often simple, plain and inexpensive to maintain, for the most part had bleachers for the fans. One of the biggest baseball events was in October after the 1928 World Series. Babe Ruth and Lou Gehrig billed as "Busting Babe" and "Larruping Lou" came to play an exhibition game at Sodality Park in San Jose. That was a memorable event!

When this old, 1926 photo was dusted, a four letter word was clearly printed on the fence. Thanks to modern technology, the word is not shown here.

Reed Field
1926

COLLEGIATE BASEBALL AND ATTRACTING THE SCOUTS

*1928 Santa Clara College
1st Baseman*

After graduation from Bellarmine College Preparatory, Marv enrolled, on a scholarship, at Santa Clara College, now Santa Clara University, becoming a first baseman for the Broncos under Coach Justin Fitzgerald, a former player for the San Francisco Seals. To quote a local sportswriter, J.A.B. in the San Jose Mercury Herald, "He is rounding out into the classiest first sacker... It's Marvin's batting average that draws plenty of attention.... Triples, doubles, and singles went on the books for the San Jose youngster... His mark, .391, stands out like a torch in the dark. Owen was this year (1928) selected by Coach Justin Fitzgerald in his all-star team and the San Jose lad deserves the place, ...was probably the most valuable player on the 1928 Bronco nine." Two of Marv's closest buddies on the team were Johnny Casanova and Guido Simoni, both pitchers. While playing for Santa Clara, Johnny Casanova and Marv, though not paid, also played for the San Mateo Blues and San Jose. This developed into a problem.

Here is the letter Marv received from his college baseball coach, "Fitz".

June 10,/28.
Dear Marv.

Just rec'd a letter from Father McCoy, saying that if Cas were to play with San Mateo, he would forfeit his collegiate standing. As you have played with San Jose, I would suggest you find out how you stand. If for any reason they place the ban on you, and you decide you want to play Prof ball, do not sign with any one until I see you, as I can do more, and can get better conditions than anyone else.
You should finish your schooling by all means, even tho you would not be eligible, as you are young and you really should be more mutured (sic) to play Prof Ball. It is quite a strain playing every day and while there would be a question at this time if you could make good, in a couple of years with added weight and experience you would be ready.
Let me hear from you soon Marv. See Walsh, and get the dope.

Sincerely

"Fitz"
1207 Palm Ave. San Mateo, CA

Consolidated Laundry Team
Fifth from left is Marv Owen; seventh is Art "Mike" Hunt, former Pacific Coast League Player.

MARVIN OWEN, BRONCO FIRST SACKER, DECLARED COLLEGE LEAGUE'S MOST VALUABLE PLAYER

In order to stay eligible for the collegiate league, the three college stars had to turn in their resignations to the semi-pro league.

On the college team Marv always played first base and was one of the best lead off hitters. He attracted the attention of many baseball scouts and club owners: Roy Mack, Ira F. Thomas, Connie Mack, C.C. Slapnicka, Bill Klepper and others. Some of their correspondence is here.

One coach said that Connie Mack offered to pay Owen's way through Harvard plus $1000.00 if he'd sign with the Philadelphia Athletics, but Marv preferred to stay and graduate at Santa Clara. The San Francisco Mission Reds' manager, Nick Williams "liked that boy, Owen," too.

Connie Mack
(Thanks to: Rev. Jerome C.C. Romanowski, Holy Name Society)

Ira F. Thomas sent this letter to Marv from Philadelphia.

Bustleton
Phila, Pa
Jan 10th '27

Dear Friend,

So glad to hear from you. I have reported to Mr. Mack many nice things about you, and I feel safe in saying when the time comes for you to take up base ball as a profession, you will make good, providing you get connected with the right manager at the beginning. Don't forget what I told you about Mr. C. Mack and get with him if you have a chance. I spoke to Roy Mack, who was at my home last week, regarding you. Roy is with Portland ball club.

Portland trains at San Jose again this year. I will have these bats sent on to your home. I expect to be at our ball Park in a day or two now and will see they get started on the way to you. I can not add in this letter more than I told you while at your home. Be a good boy, don't do wrong to be smart, like so many boys do. Listen to your Mother and Father, they are your truest friends and will help you to do right. Talk your little troubles over with them. Listen to your baseball coach. He has had lots of experience and has a good reputation.

Write me once in awhile, and send me clippings of your work at school. I will close now trusting the bats reach you OK. I remain

Your friend,

Ira F. Thomas *

*Catcher for Detroit and Philadelphia in the American League from 1906 through 1915.

Santa Clara College Student
1928, San Jose, California

PORTLAND BASE BALL CLUB
PACIFIC COAST LEAGUE
24TH AND VAUGHN STREETS PORTLAND, OREGON

THOMAS L. TURNERGUS. C. MOSER
President-TreasurerSecretary
ROY F. MACKERNIE JOHNSON
Vice-Pres.-Bus. Mgr.Manager

June 6, 1928

Dear Marvin:

On account of being so busy have not been able to find time to write to you. Mr. Turner made a hurried getaway for the East so I was called home from Seattle. Our club has not been going very good so it is Mr. Turner's intention to strengthen for the second half. I spoke to him about placing you in semi pro ball where you could play three or four games per week. He had in mind the Butte Mine League as the only semi pro league playing that many week day games. He also thought that you might sign a contract and enter pro ball. The Mine League as I understand is not playing this year. So you still want to go to college, think it advisable for you to play as near home as possible. Whenever you are ready to play pro ball you can let me know. We would like to have you on our club and no doubt will not have any difficulties as to terms.

We play the Seals next week and I would like to have you come up to see the games. I will no doubt make the trip but my doctor wants me to be operated on for a very bad hernia. I am trying to put it off until the fall. With kind personal regards to your mother and you, I am

Sincerely Yours

Roy F. Mack*

*One of Connie Mack's sons.

WESTERN UNION

Sept. 1929

THE CLEVELAND CLUB WILL MAIL YOU CHECK THIRTY FIVE HUNDRED IMMEDIATELY UPON RECEIPT OF YOUR SIGNED AGREEMENT STOP WIRE ACCEPTANCE TO ME COLLECT TONIGHT AT TEXAS HOTEL FTWORTH TEXAS NIGHTLETTER STOP I WILL MAIL AGREEMENT FROM THERE WILL BE FTWORTH TOMORROW ONLY=

C C SLAPNICKA.*

C. C. Slapnicka of the Cleveland Indians telegraphed this tempting offer. It was also turned down. Seattle's Bill Klepper was interested in Marv and persistently kept his eye on him. Six or more rival scouts or club owners made offers but none were accepted until after Marv graduated from Santa Clara in May 1930.

At the end of the 1929 baseball season, Marv was elected to Captain the 1930 Santa Clara baseball team. Coach Justin Fitzgerald said of him, "He was undoubtedly the most valuable man in the California Intercollegiate Baseball Association. He was a quick thinker and did the right thing at the right time." However, when the baseball season opened, he was declared ineligible to play his senior year because he had agreed to sign after graduation with the Seattle Club in the Pacific Coast League even though Seattle tried to intervene.

WESTERN UNION

Nov. 1929

MARVIN OWEN., SANTA CLARA COLLEGE
MR. KLEPPER ON WAY EAST WILL NOT BE BACK UNTIL DECEMBER FIFTEENTH STOP WIRE ME WHAT COLLEGE OFFICIAL OR PARTY YOU WANT ME TO TAKE MATTER UP WITH AND I WILL GET BUSY BY WIRE AND TRY STRAIGHTEN MATTER OUT BY ADVISING THAT NEITHER OF YOU HAVE AS YET SIGNED PROFESSIONAL CONTRACT YOU HAVE ONLY GIVEN YOUR WORD IN WRITING THAT YOU WILL SIGN AFTER YOU ARE THROUGH SCHOOL WHICH SHOULD NOT DISQUALIFY YOUR AMATEUR STANDING

FRED B RIVERS,
SECRETARY SEATTLE BASEBALL CLUB

*This is the same C.C.Slapnicka who, in 1936, signed Bob Feller for the Cleveland Indians.

As Buddy Leitch wrote in his San Jose News column at that time, "when he graduates in May, with a record to be proud of – not only as a coach and scholar, but that of a true sportsman who had enough intestinal fortitude to fight his way back to the top after he had fallen for an unreasonable trick which robbed him of his amateur standing and for a time marked him as an outcast. The college authorities appointed him the 1930 varsity baseball coach where successfully he coached his former teammates." (He was the youngest baseball coach at the time.) Fifty-three years later, in 1983, the Santa Clara University Baseball Yearbook was dedicated to him.

Graduation from Santa Clara College
May 1930

In reminiscing many years later (2-20-43) Bill Klepper was quoted in "Buddy" Leitch's column in the San Jose Evening News "It was here (in the Sainte Claire Hotel in San Jose) that I signed Marv (Freck) Owen to his first professional contract. Marv was considered one of the greatest prospects in college history. He had all kinds of offers, so many as a matter of fact that he was in a position to write his own ticket but I finally landed him on the terms of $2000.00 when he signed the contract and an additional $2000.00 on the day he joined the Seattle Club. That was big dough to put out to an untried college kid but I figured he was worth the gamble. He reported to Seattle in June, 1930 after graduation from S.C. and in less than a full season with Seattle, his contract was transferred to Detroit in 1931 for something like $40,000.00. Anyway, I got $25,000.00 in cash and the balance in two players. Anyway, it was one of the sweetest deals I ever swung. Not only that, but Marv was a sound performer in every respect, his years of service under the big tent proving me a good judge of talent in the rough."
At that time Pacific Coast League teams rarely had working agreements with major league teams. They signed their own players and made money selling their players to the majors.

*The Philadelphia Athletics and the Portland Beavers had been outbid by the Seattle Indians.

II. ON THE TRAIL OF A TIGER— WHAT IT WAS LIKE TO BE A PRO

*Marv signs with Seattle Pacific
Coast League, 1930*

When Marv joined the Seattle Indians, June 1930, in his first professional season, he had just graduated from Santa Clara College. Basically, he was a shy, small town (San Jose), young man with little experience of being away from home, living in a hotel with a roommate, or meeting all kinds of new people. He confessed to his sister, Evelyn, at the time, that he was excited at the prospect of playing pro ball, but the other aspects made him nervous as he anticipated what was ahead. However, he never doubted his baseball capabilities.

INDIANS FIND GEM IN OWEN

THE YOUNG Santa Clara collegiate, Marv Owen, now with the Indians, put on a display of shortstopping Tuesday night that drew considerable comment. Owen originally was a firstbaseman, where he starred for the Broncos, but in an emergency Ernie Johnson had to shift the youngster to the left side of the field and now he's making a strong bid for the position. He is being picked over Muller, although the latter is considered a better hitter, while Chick Ellsworth, the regular, is on the sick list. Owen turned in several hard plays the opening night and seems to possess all the qualifications of an outstanding recruit.

"I want to give the boy a few day's rest," said Ernie Johnson, "but I can't seem to find a chance to do it. The youngster has played almost every day since joining our club a month ago and he's not used to every day play. He hasn't had any spring training except the short time he played in college during the spring and the grind may be too hard for him at the start."

The first week Owen joined the Indians in San Francisco he was played at first, second, third and short on four successive days. He will be a valuable man to the club in a year or so.

In the first month playing for Seattle, he had little rest and he had not had any spring training. The first week with the Seattle Indians he played first, second, third, and short on four successive days. In his first ten days at first base, he maintained a perfect fielding average of 1.000. Then, the shortstop, Chick Ellsworth, broke a shoulder bone, so Marv played short for the next 45 games and had a fielding average of .948. According to newspaper reports, he proved himself a remarkable infielder, clutch hitter, "with a wonderful arm, plenty of nerve, a fine pair of hands and legs that carry him over the ground at a rapid rate..." He was in the Coast League less than a week when a major league club offered $25,000. for him (not accepted!).

Santa Clara Youngster Steps Into Fullerton's Pitch to Win Thriller

Great 15-Inning Battle Ended as Rookie Singles; Boy's Record With Indians Is Something to Marvel Over

THE Portland Beavers have discovered "Freck" Owen.

With the sun shining thru the back of the grandstand, good hot dinners burning up and housewives berating their absent hubbies late Tuesday afternoon, "Freck" steeped up and broke up a 15-inning ball game.

For 14 innings the Beavers had had his number. He'd been to bat six times without the semblance of a hit, the longest stretch of inactivity from the task of building a batting average he'd been thru since he joined the Indians.

The Beavers had him figured as a straightaway hitter—right, too—and were playing him in a funnel-shaped formation that left great gaps back of first and third bases but which closed up the territory in which Owen had been hitting.

A foul fly to first base and four crashing drives to the outfield had been gathered in to stop the boy. He'd reached first once when his poorest-hit ball of the day eluded Ossie Orwoll.

But Freck wasn't thru by any means. In the 15th Fritz Knothe singled to right, was sacrificed along, held second while Dutch Holland was waved out on a fly to center and while Louis Almada was purposely passed.

That "insult" was too much. Freck gritted his teeth and banged the second strike thrown him thru the pitcher's box and into center field to score Knothe from second with the winning run. Seattle had won the longest game of the year here, 15 innings, by a 6-5 score.

* * *

This boy is a pip.

Do you know that since he was shifted to first base, his natural position, he hasn't made an error?

How many college boys ever broke into Class A baseball without committing at least a few errors in their first games? Not many!

Freck has not only made every mechanical play right but he's made every mental play that has confronted him the way it should be made.

He's shifting for batters, trying to hit behind runners, listening to his boss and bearing down.

What a boy!

On July 5, 1930, Marv received a telegram from his first coach and mentor, his dad. "Congratulations on your first homerun." J.Owen

After his first and only season with Seattle, Marv was sold to the Detroit Tigers for $25,000 plus two players. An astonishing deal for that time, maybe even a record!

In 1931, San Jose again had placed a baseball player into the major leagues – Hal Chase, Hal Rhyne and now, Marv Owen went to the majors.

Marvin Owen

Marvin Owen Is Sold to Detroit

Marvin "Freck" Owen is going up.

The former Santa Clara university baseball star and coach, who has been playing sensational ball for the Seattle Indians at shortstop and first base during the present season, has become the property of the Detroit Tigers, according to the Associated Press.

Owen has been outstanding as a Seattle hitter, his average having been up to the .300 mark. He has likewise been regarded as one of the cleanest fielders in the Pacific coast loop. He joined the Tribe this spring following a season as coach of the Santa Clara Broncos.

Marvin Owen Former Seattle Infielder, Camp's Leading Recruit

Marvin Owen, the San Jose youth who sparkled for the Seattle Indians last season, coming from the Santa Clara nine, joined the Tigers to-day. Owen was one of the best young infielders who has entered the coast league for many years, and his coming to the Tigers is creating more than a little interest among the Detroit officials. Owen is certain to make some of the infield recruits or veterans hustle to hold their jobs. Marvin was good enough to draw a $25,000 bid from the Cleveland Indians after being in the coast league less than two weeks.

23

Joining the Tigers in 1931, Marv was the young, still shy, unseasoned player who had had only about four months of professional experience playing for the Seattle Indians of the Coast League. Many years later in describing how shy he was when he was called up by the Tigers he told a reporter, "I was so shy as a rookie I used a bat that was too big because I was afraid to ask for a smaller one." It is not surprising that he was farmed out to Toronto and then Newark in his first year with Detroit....

The question may be raised, "How could he be farmed out to two different clubs in one season?" This letter from Marv explains.

"Dear Jack,

After being shipped from Detroit to Toronto and then to Newark, I believe it is about time to write to you.

Detroit broke relations with Toronto which had been their farm team for four or five years and so I was farmed to Newark; this was a very fortunate break for me as I went from a tail-ender to a club in second place and now we are in first place with a six game lead and are about ready to open up a long home stay.

We just finished a road trip yesterday with 15 victories and five losses. A few of the clubs play night ball here. Newark, Buffalo and Baltimore play it once a week while Reading has it every night. The lighting system in this league is not up to Coast league standards.

I am the youngest ball player in the league. We are noted for being the fastest club and we have eight regulars hitting over .300.

After a poor start with Toronto I finally reached the .300 mark and at present am hitting .303. I started the season as shortstop with Toronto but am playing third for Newark.

The winners of this league will play the champions of the American association in "the little world's series" at the end of the season and it now appears that our club will be the champs of this league. Our entire outfit is trying hard to win as it means a little extra money if we get in the championship series.

I was glad to hear that "Happy Luke" Williams was again running a ball team. I know it's been tough for Luke to be without a club the last few years but now things will be O.K. with him.

Well, Jack, I hope your leagues are going along fine. They can't help but be a success with you at the helm.

Meanwhile I'm waiting for the end of the season so that I can give the east back to the eastern people and I'll take California for mine. Give my regards to all the boys.

Your friend,

MARVIN OWEN.

In his one season, 1932, with the Newark Bears of the International League, Marv was described as a marvelous defensive player (now including 3rd base, as well as 1st and shortstop), a stout clubber in the clutches, an aggressive hustler and responsible for steadying the infield.

Light hitting in 1931 at Detroit was one of the factors that sent Marv to the minors for seasoning.

In September 1931 after playing 105 games for Detroit, only hitting .223 and fielding .937, the Detroit management allowed Marv to return early to San Jose, CA. One of his sisters had been critically injured in an accident in California and had been hospitalized. He went home immediately to see his sister and to be with his family.

Marv plays 3rd for Newark
International League

The Old Sauce

"I can pitch or play the outfield,
  On the infield I'm at home;
I can catch as good as any,
And I always use my dome.

"I can hit like Ruth or Gehrig,
  I can run like Tyrus Cobb;
And when it comes to bunting
  I'm far from any slob.

"I can work the hit and run play,
  I can sacrifice with ease;
I'm a reg'lar hornet's stinger
  In putting on the squeeze.

"I can cover ground and get 'em,
  I can throw like rifle shot;
What it takes to be a season's find
  Is just the stuff I've got."

Thus spoke the budding rookie,
  In talking to his boss;
Who listened with attentive ear,
  Then muttered "apple sauce."

"The Old Sauce" was an
anonymous poem kept by
Marv in his book of
favorite clippings
(Source unknown)

Early Years League Records

Yr	Club	League	G.	AB.	R.	H.	HR.	SB.	Pat.	PO.	A	E.	Ave.
1930	Seattle	P.C.L.	138	443	67	133	3	16	.300	400	342	22	.971
1931	Toronto	I.L.	37	131	18	41	0	1	.313	36	55	5	.948
1931	Detroit	A.L.	105	377	35	84	3	2	.223	299	206	24	.955
1932	Tor./Newark	I.L.	160	587	103	186	11	13	.317	218	338	32	.952

At the very successful conclusion of the 1932 season with the Newark Bears, he was voted by the sports writers as the Most Valuable Player in the International League. One reporter wrote, "Owen was a ball player, gentleman. Owen could hit, field, throw, run the bases and play any position in the infield. He was especially brilliant under fire. He hit when hits meant the most. He grabbed 'em out of the dirt and whipped the ball across the diamond like a bullet.... He was that kind of a ballplayer." The voting poll was sponsored in the minor league by the Sporting News for the first time in baseball history. Newark clinched the pennant that year and Marv finished the season with a batting average of .321. He was recalled to Detroit for 1933!

Marv receives The Sporting News Award and Trophy from John Smith, former Mayor of Detroit, at home plate, Navin Field, June 22, 1934.
(Credit: The Sporting News)

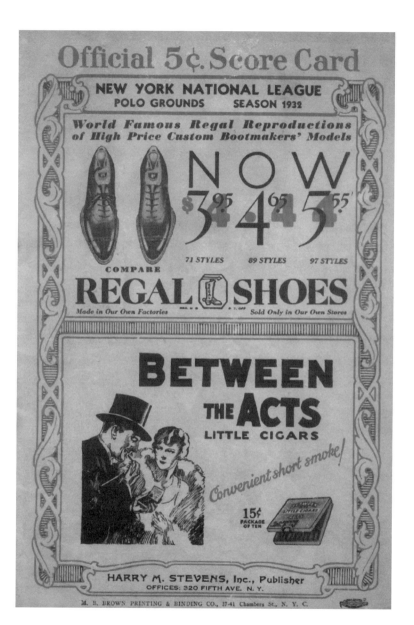

Marv plays an exhibition game in 1932 at the Polo Grounds.
New York- National League
Detroit- American League

Throughout his life Marv had a singlemindedness: baseball. When he arrived as a regular pro with the Detroit Tigers, he gained self-confidence as he pursued his lifelong ambition, but he was still shy and not much of a talker. Beginning in the first season of his professional life, he found expression in writing letters.

Words were important to him whether it was writing a letter home, which he did often, writing to a friend, doing a crossword puzzle or writing poetry. All·of these became hobbies that lasted all his life. Even into his eighties he continued his correspondence with Charlie Gehringer and Billy Rogell and continued to enjoy writing poetry and solving word puzzles.

As a rookie (1st year in Majors) all major leaguers I did fear.
Later I was as good as any and had no peer.
Was not big headed, just confident,
Knew when the ball came to me–I'd catch it,
throw it, hitter would be out
Back to the dugout he'd be sent.

M.O.

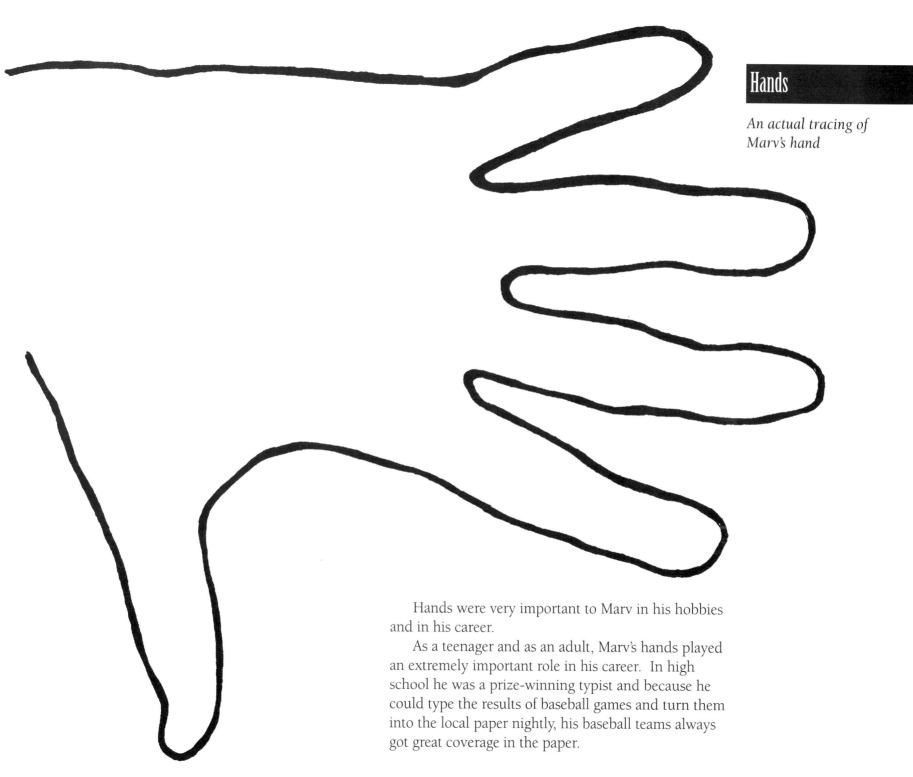

Hands

An actual tracing of Marv's hand

Hands were very important to Marv in his hobbies and in his career.

As a teenager and as an adult, Marv's hands played an extremely important role in his career. In high school he was a prize-winning typist and because he could type the results of baseball games and turn them into the local paper nightly, his baseball teams always got great coverage in the paper.

29

In 1928 he was able to hold seven regulation baseballs in each hand with palms straight up and could turn the balls facing down. For this he was pictured in "Believe It Or Not" by Ripley. The glove that held the 7 balls was sent to be displayed at the Cooperstown Hall of Fame and Museum in 1978.

When he was playing for Detroit, F.S. Nixon, a newspaper cartoonist called him a "ham hand at third."

This feat was noted in Believe It or Not by Ripley

©1995 Ripley Entertainment Inc.
Registered Trademark of Ripley Entertainment Inc.

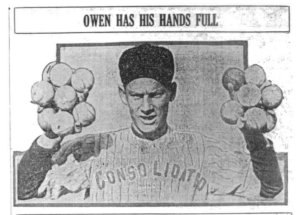

May 23, 1928
(credit: San Jose Mercury)

When he began professional baseball his hands were described like this:
- ham hands
- methodical
- enormous
- steady
- abnormally large
- surest fielding
- powerful
- accurate
- strong
- high class
- man-sized
- one of finest pair of hands in baseball.

His hands helped him to achieve outstanding fielding records in the Pacific Coast League with Seattle and later Portland, and with Detroit in the American League. In 1936, with Detroit, he had a fielding average of .970, the best fielding average for a third baseman in the league that year.

When both Hank Greenberg and Marv were rookies with Detroit, Greenberg looked to Marv for tips on how to catch fly balls. Hank had been catching flies with his hands raised above his head. He watched Marv take a fly ball at about waist high and smother the ball in his large hands. Hank practiced this method and made it his.

The great 1934 Tiger infield, Greenberg at 1st, Gehringer at 2nd, Rogell at shortstop, Owen at 3rd, all fielded over .950.

Marv's Glove
(Photo Credit: Herb Quinn, WA)

MARV OWEN

SUREST HANDS — Few third basemen are as sure on ground balls as Marvin Owen. He has a pair of exceptionally large hands and a remarkable throwing arm. He is a timely hitter and better than ordinary base runner. He has completely recovered from the poor health that handicapped him earlier in the season. He has been playing sensationally of late. Detroit Times Photo.

(reprinted with permission of the Detroit News)

In the Detroit years of the '30s, who could imagine a better infield than Charley Gehringer at 2nd, Hank Greenberg at 1st, Marv Owen at 3rd, and Billy Rogell at shortstop, better pitchers than Schoolboy Rowe, Tommy Bridges, Eldon Auker, better fielders than "Goose" Goslin, "Jo-Jo White, "Pete" Fox, and Gerry Walker, a great catcher like Ray Hayworth, and a better player/manager than Mickey Cochrane?

What was it like to travel, to play, to eat, to talk to such a group of teammates? Good fortune was with Marv. Hank Greenberg, Charley Gehringer and Billy Rogell, who were to become Marv's good friends, all shared something in common. The four infielders were outstanding in their respective playing positions, they were all intelligent, they were all gentle men. Each one respected the talents and abilities of the others. There was not a "showboat" in the group. They enjoyed playing the game together.

The four infielders became friends off the field as well as on. Charlie, Hank and Marv were single and Billy Rogell was married. When the team played home games, Charlie lived at home in Detroit, Billy and his wife had an apartment and Marv and Hank lived at the Wolverine Hotel (Wolf House) in Detroit.

Marv loved to dance. When he was especially happy and wanted to display his happiness, he had a little tap dance that was his routine. It was something to behold: six foot one and one half and 170 lbs. doing a buck and wing. He predated Deion Sanders! Off the field, Marv and Hank, a Jew, would often go stag to dances, alternating one time going to a dance where Jewish girls were and then going to a dance where Gentile girls were. Hank turned to Marv when he had to make a decision whether to play on Rosh Hashanah or not. Marv's policy was make a good first decision and then no second guessing.

Big Hank Greenberg's bat kept games alive
His number was five.
Number 7 was Billy Rogell,
At shortstop he did excel.
The San Jose kid on 3rd was number 8
To the hot corner he was never late.
Goose Goslin in left field was number 4
He added to the Tiger lore.
Gerry Walker's number was 6
Running bases got him in a tight fix.
Pitcher Auker's number was 13
No jinx, in fact, he thought it was keen.
Little Tommy Bridges' number was 10
I'd like to see that hurler pitch again.

M.O.

Tommy Bridges
(Credit: National Baseball Library and Archive, Cooperstown, N.Y.)

Gee Walker, Detroit Outfielder
1934 at Lakeland, Florida, Tiger Training Camp
(Credit: ACME/Bettmann)

Gerry Walker, able, popular and colorful outfielder for Detroit in the '30s was a free spirit. At one game in Chicago when it was extremely cold in the dugout, Gerry took the matter into his own hands and started a small campfire in the dugout. Naturally, officials put out the fire and Gerry took some heat.

At another time after the conclusion of a game, it was shower time. As Marv was going to take his, he was surprised to see Gee Walker and his two little sons showering together.

It seems after the game Walker was taking off his uniform when his two small sons walked over to his locker. He said, "Mike and Pat do you want to take a shower with me and the players?" They answered in the affirmative, so the three of them took off their clothes, went in their birthday suits into the shower room to take a shower.

Gee was noted for his erratic base running (always getting picked off). During the series in St. Louis, his family was left behind in Detroit. His 2 small children - age 3 and 4 were in Detroit; their mother did not have the radio on, but the kids could hear the game on the radio from across the street. All of a sudden the radio announcer bellowed out, "He's picked off first base." One of the small kids said to Mrs Walker, "Was that my father?"

Bases loaded, Marv was hitting with no count; all of a sudden while the pitcher is winding up to pitch, Goslin breaks for 3rd base — and Marv noticed that there was already a runner on 3rd; the pitch was a foot over his head; luck was on his side and he singled to center. To get Goslin off the hook, they told their teammates the "hit and run" play was on — which was a white lie. Goose was quoted as saying "It's a lucky thing Owen hit that single through there or the Goose would have looked bad and I don't like to look like a chump, not at my age."

In St. Louis versus the Browns, the Tigers were fighting for a pennant. Marv was hitting and was given the bunt signal with Goslin on 2nd, Gee Walker on 1st base. First pitch to Marv was a ball; catcher threw the ball to 1st baseman, and Gee was caught in a rundown, and was chased to 2nd base, where Goslin was caught in a rundown, and finally tagged out with Gee getting to second base. Marv grounded out to short with Gee holding 2nd base — before the next hitter had a pitch made to him, Gee was picked off second, the pitcher to the second baseman, which retired the side. The Tigers got the Browns out. On the way to the dugout Goslin (lf) said to Walker (rf) as the three approached the dugout "What in the hell were you thinking about on those bases?" Gee answered, "You big nosed so and so, mind your own business." Then Cochrane, the manager, stepped in and said "That stupid baserunning will cost you 50 dollars." Gee said, "Make it a hundred." Cochrane answered, "It will be 200 and go to the clubhouse and change your clothes."

Hank Greenberg, Charlie Gehringer and Marvin Owen, three "good-will ambassadors" for their team and for baseball, visit a service club after playing a doubleheader against the Boston Red Sox in Detroit.

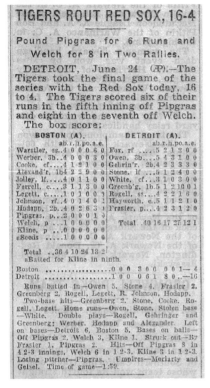

TIGERS ROUT RED SOX, 16-4

Pound Pipgras for 6 Runs and Welch for 8 in Two Rallies.

DETROIT, June 24 (AP).—The Tigers took the final game of the series with the Red Sox today, 16 to 4. The Tigers scored six of their runs in the fifth inning off Pipgras and eight in the seventh off Welch. The box score:

A really good day,
June 25, 1933

The New York Times Sunday June 25, 1933 caption declared "Tiger Rout Red Sox 16-4". In the game played in Detroit on the 24th Marv had a really good day, hitting 3 for 5, scoring four times, batting in 5 runs, making one putout and no errors, and hitting one home run.

When Marv was an unseasoned, third baseman playing for Detroit, Charlie Gehringer, experienced 2nd baseman for the team, never said anything on the field when they were playing. One day when Marv was sent in to play shortstop, he and Charlie both went after a pop fly. In the resulting collision Marv stepped on Charlie and spiked his toe. Marv recalled that Charlie said, "I can catch a fly ball if it isn't too high, so will you please stay on your own side of second base after this?" That was the first time Charlie had talked to Marv. However, off the field Marv and Charlie became life-long friends, both real gentlemen, quiet and with great good humor. Many years later Charlie and Marv attended the 1968 Tigers/Cardinals World Series and Marv, from California, had not brought an overcoat. Charlie loaned him one of his overcoats to wear during the series. A few months later he sent Marv the camel hair overcoat that Marv had previously borrowed. In with the gift was this card from Charlie.

Dear Marv,
This little present is for stepping on my foot back in good years.
Wear it in good health especially the Series in '69???

Charlie

During one of the few times Gehringer was in a slump, he said "I could foul out if I played in an elevator shaft."

From the first time they met and played in the Tiger infield in 1933, Charlie Gehringer was always "Chollie" to Marv. Both players were quiet, serious, disciplined and had great subtle humor. They enjoyed each other on and off the field. Marv really looked up to Chollie and respected his great ability.

In 1938 when Marv and Violet Walsh were married in Detroit, Chollie was the best man. Eleven years later in 1949, when Charlie Gehringer and Josephine Stillen planned their wedding, Marv and his wife in Santa Clara, California, made the arrangements for the couple to be wed quietly in Santa Clara at Saint Clare's Church. However, the newspapers found out about it. In order to give Chollie and Jo the privacy they desired, Marv and his wife, Violet, as best man and matron of honor, took the betrothed couple with the priest to St. Patrick's Church in San Jose where the ceremony was quiet and private.

Meanwhile back at Cooperstown, New York, Chollie was among the missing. He had been named to Cooperstown Hall of Fame and the day of enshrinement was the same day as the wedding. When news of the wedding was announced, everyone agreed he had good reason to miss Cooperstown! (Marv always saved the letter he received on April 7, 1949 from Chollie detailing plans for the California June wedding.)

Charlie Gehringer details plans for his wedding to Josephine Stillen in a letter to Marv.

Groom to be: Charlie Gehringer
Best Man to be: Marv Owen
Santa Clara, CA 1949
(Thanks to: Mrs. Charles L. Gehringer)

Years later when St. Patrick's Church was torn down, Marv sent one of the bricks to Chollie and Jo. Many years later in 1989 in a letter to Marv, Jo wrote, "You asked if we have the St. Patrick's Church brick. Yes, we do and it is prominently displayed on the mantle in our family room."

If you look at films of baseball games of the '30s, you'll see many differences compared to baseball games today.

- In the '30s, baseball was Number 1! It was the Golden Age of Baseball!
- The bats are different today. The balls are different; they're livelier. Today the players wear batting gloves. Some wear ear protectors. Some wear leg, knee or wrist braces.
- The players' uniforms fit like tight socks. I'm glad I never had to wear them! Our uniforms were wool.
- There was no beer in the clubhouse.
- There were no mustaches or beards.
- When we received our instructions before going to spring training among the written rules were these: no wives and no cars!
- In the thirties, radio was the major way of carrying baseball games. Today television is the medium. When you listened to a game on the radio, you had to use your imagination and do your visualization. The announcers did, too.
- A show off was a "showboat." Now that behavior is "hot doggin." There were no "high fives." There was no "bashing."
- Today, the professional baseball players' organization is very strong. Players have individual agents. Negotiating salaries is now an art. In the thirties each player negotiated his own contract. Today, there are many kinds of bonuses.
- No one was on drugs, but there were a few who drank too much.
- The salaries for the 30's were good for the 30's, but they would be peanuts for the 90's. In 1931 my contract was $625.00 a month which was good for a beginner. There were no multi-year contracts. These were depression years. In 1972 the average

salary was $34,092. Today hundreds of professional baseball players make multimillions per year. The average salary in 1992 was $1,028,667. Barry Bonds has a 5 year contract for over 43 million dollars.

- Here are samples of World Series shares:
  1935 Tigers winners take: $6831.88 each;
  Cubs losers take: $4382.72 each.
  1936 Total World Series gross receipts Grand Total: $1,304,399.00; Detroit: second place share: $34,500.20 - $1254.55 (each player).
  1937 Total World Series gross receipts Grand Total: $1,085,944.00; Detroit: second place share: $34,472.20 - $1188.70 (each player).
- When I was playing, the players were identified by the numbers on their uniforms. Now each is identified with his name on his uniform.
- Some of the present day players keep in shape at health spas to participate in weight lifting and body building. Instead of weight lifting I chopped wood, ran the local college track and kept in shape playing catch and hitting fungoes with my dad. This was even after I entered professional ball.
- An improvement of the present time is the player's helmet. A blow to the head is no fun.
- In my time I never asked kids to pay for my autograph. Now with the card shows, signing autographs is big business.
- We played when we were in pain, seldom missing a game.
- There were sixteen teams.
- When we traveled in the 30's, we went by bus or train. We never flew. The following schedule gives you an idea of how we traveled, how far, how often and how fast. It also shows where we stayed.

Detroit Baseball Company

BULLETIN

LAKELAND, FLORIDA

March 1, 1936

BUS MOVES VIA FLORIDA MOTOR LINES

Date	Day	City	Mileage Round Trip	Running Time Each Way
March 12	Thursday	Tampa	70	1 Hour
March 15	Sunday	Clearwater	140	2 Hours
March 16	Monday	St. Petersburg	110	1¾ Hours
March 17	Tuesday	Lake Wales	70	1 Hour
March 18	Wednesday	Orlando	140	2 Hours
March 21	Saturday	Clearwater	140	2 Hours
March 26	Thursday	Bradenton	160	2 Hours
March 28	Saturday	Sarasota	190	2¾ Hours
March 29	Sunday	Tampa	70	1 Hour

(Bulletins will be posted in club house relative to time of departure of buses on the moves outlined above and those making different trips. Lunch and Dinner allowance credited in all of these cities. Information for Detroit office:—Club returns to Hotel Lakeland Terrace, Lakeland, each night on these Bus trips.)

Thur.	April 9	Lv. Durham	Southern Ry.	No. 13	7:12 P.M.
Thur.	April 9	Ar. Greensboro	Southern Ry.	No. 13	8:50 P.M.
Thur.	April 9	Lv. Greensboro	Southern Ry.	No. 38	9:50 P.M.
Fri.	April 10	Ar. Lynchburg	Southern Ry.	No. 38	12:25 A.M.
Fri.	April 10	Lv. Lynchburg	Ches. & Ohio	(Spec.)	12:30 A.M.
Fri.	April 10	Ar. Clifton Forge	Ches. & Ohio	(Spec.)	3:50 A.M.
Fri.	April 10	Lv. Clifton Forge	Ches. & Ohio	No. 3	4:50 A.M.
Fri.	April 10	Ar. Charleston	Ches. & Ohio	No. 3	9:45 A.M.

(Mileage—427 Miles)

Fri.	April 10	Lv. Charleston	Ches. & Ohio	No. 5	10:38 P.M.
Sat.	April 11	Ar. Cincinnati	Ches. & Ohio	No. 5	7:30 A.M.
Sat.	April 11	Lv. Cincinnati	Big Four Ry.	No. 146	9:00 A.M.
Sat.	April 11	Ar. Dayton	Big Four Ry.	No. 146	10:14 A.M.

(Mileage—267 Miles)

Sat.	April 11	Lv. Dayton	Big Four Ry.	No. 35	7:45 P.M.
Sat.	April 11	Ar. Cincinnati	Big Four Ry.	No. 35	9:10 P.M.

(Mileage—55 Miles)

Sun.	April 12	Lv. Cincinnati	Big Four Ry.	No. 42	11:50 P.M.
Mon.	April 13	Ar. Columbus	Big Four Ry.	No. 42	3:15 A.M.
Mon.	April 13	Lv. Columbus	Big Four Ry.	No. 42	3:25 A.M.
Mon.	April 13	Ar. Cleveland	Big Four Ry.	No. 42	7:30 A.M.

(Mileage—262 Miles)

Thur.	April 16	Lv. Cleveland	N. Y. Central	No. 43	5:35 P.M.
Thur.	April 16	Ar. Toledo	N. Y. Central	No. 43	7:57 P.M.
Thur.	April 16	Lv. Toledo	Mich. Central	No. 228	8:05 P.M.
Thur.	April 16	Ar. Detroit	Mich. Central	No. 228	9:36 P.M.

(Mileage—165 Miles)

The above schedule listed for your information and convenience at this time is subject to change. In the event of a change, notice will be given a day previous to our departure.

American League Schedule posted in Club House.

Checking out of Lakeland Terrace Hotel at 10:00 A. M., Friday, April 3 (after breakfast), Lunch (April 3) included in allowance given for trip North.

Information regarding Pullman assignments and car numbers will be announced by Trainer Carroll at depot on day of our departure.

Dining Cars on Trains No. 92 and No. 74, Lakeland to Savannah.

Monday—April 13
Club Workout at 2:00 P. M., League Park, Cleveland

Players' Schedule Spring 1936

CHANGES IN EXHIBITION SCHEDULE

Tuesday, April 7, Detroit vs. Cincinnati Nationals at Gastonia, North Carolina
Saturday, April 11, Detroit vs. Cincinnati Nationals at Dayton, Ohio
(Charlotte, North Carolina, and Portsmouth, Ohio, listed on these dates in the original training schedule.)

PERSONAL TRUNKS

Will leave camp Tuesday, March 31—Checked through to Detroit. Our baggage trucks will leave the Lakeland Terrace Hotel at 7:30 P. M. on that date. If you have a personal trunk in camp, kindly notify Trainer Carroll so that a record may be made of same. Give room number and number of trunks.

HOTELS

CITY	NAME
Lakeland	Lakeland Terrace
Tampa	Floridan
Clearwater	Fort Harrison
St. Petersburg	Detroit
Lake Wales	Dixie Walesbilt
Orlando	San Juan
Bradenton	Dixie Grande
Sarasota	Sarasota Terrace
Gastonia	Armington
Dayton	Van Cleve

(Consult original player roster and schedule for hotel headquarters in other cities.)

(Pay your extra charges before your departure from hotel. Inquire at Cashier's window if any extra charges are posted against your room. Sometimes a charge is made through error.)

BAGGAGE TRANSFER ORGANIZATIONS

CITY	NAME
Lakeland	Yarnell Transfer Company
Columbia	Checker Cab Company
Augusta	Augusta Cab & Transfer Co.
Florence	Privette Mozingo
Charlotte	Charlotte Transfer Company
Winston Salem	Hotel Robert E. Lee
Durham	Blue Bird Taxicab Company
Charleston	Jordan Taxi Company
Dayton	Union Station Transfer Co.
Cincinnati	Cincinnati Railroad Omnibus Co.

TAXICABS

The Detroit Baseball Company will not be responsible for the payment of taxicab charge accounts between hotels and depots for the reason that an allowance is given for all movements of this kind. It recognizes and honors accounts of this nature only when the players are dressed in uniform and going to and from the ball grounds.

HAND BAGGAGE

Detraining in every city each man is responsible for own hand baggage. Checking out of every hotel a truck will be provided for hand baggage—hotel to depot. Please do not leave coats and hats or other personal belongings on top of hand baggage—outgoing—the baggage transfer organizations will not assume responsibility on these articles mentioned For the reason that our cars are engaged on an overflow basis—and not chartered or private—hand baggage must be removed as we detrain—the Pullman Company will not be responsible for property left in car. Detraining and entraining from the same depot and not requiring your baggage—the depot check room is recommended. See that metal tag with club name and your number is attached to your grips to properly identify same at different hotels and railroad terminals.

RAILROAD SCHEDULE

Fri.	April	3	Lv. Lakeland	Atl. Coast Line	No. 92	11:40 A.M.
Fri.	April	3	Ar. Jacksonville	Atl. Coast Line	No. 92	4:50 P.M.
Fri.	April	3	Lv. Jacksonville	Atl. Coast Line	No. 74	5:10 P.M.
Fri.	April	3	Ar. Savannah	Atl. Coast Line	No. 74	8:15 P.M.
Sat.	April	4	Lv. Savannah	Southern Ry.	No. 24	12:55 A.M.
Sat.	April	4	Ar. Columbia	Southern Ry.	No. 24	4:50 A.M.

(Mileage, 487 Miles; cars placed for occupancy until 8:00 A.M.)

Sun.	April	5	Lv. Columbia	Southern Ry.	No. 31	8:40 A.M.
Sun.	April	5	Ar. Augusta	Southern Ry.	No. 31	11:20 A.M.

(Mileage—83 Miles)

Mon.	April	6	Lv. Augusta	Atl. Coast Line	No. 54	3:15 A.M.

(Cars to be placed for occupancy, 10:00 P. M., Sunday, April 5)

Mon.	April	6	Ar. Florence	Atl. Coast Line	No. 54	8:05 A.M.

(Mileage—168 Miles)

Mon.	April	6	Lv. Florence	Atl. Coast Line	No. 65	8:20 P.M.
Mon.	April	6	Ar. Columbia	Atl. Coast Line	No. 65	10:45 P.M.
Tues.	April	7	Lv. Columbia	Southern Ry.	No. 24	5:00 A.M.
Tues.	April	7	Ar. Charlotte	Southern Ry.	No. 24	8:15 A.M.

(Mileage, 190 Miles; Bus Charlotte to Gastonia, 21 Miles)

Wed.	April	8	Lv. Charlotte	Southern Ry.	No. 24	8:35 A.M.
Wed.	April	8	Ar. Winston-Salem	Southern Ry.	No. 24	11:35 A.M.

(Mileage—83 Miles)

Thur.	April	9	Lv. Winston-Salem	Southern Ry.	No. 10	10:15 A.M.
Thur.	April	9	Ar. Greensboro	Southern Ry.	No. 10	11:00 A.M.
Thur.	April	9	Lv. Greensboro	Southern Ry.	No. 16	11:30 A.M.
Thur.	April	9	Ar. Durham	Southern Ry.	No. 16	1:10 P.M.

(Mileage—83 Miles)

Players' Schedule Spring 1936 (cont.)

When Marv was asked about contracts and regulations of the '30's, he explained with examples of the times.

"In 1931 there were no agents for the players nor was there a strong negotiating organization for the players. The negotiating was done between the player and the club owner or club president. Our contracts were one year contracts. I've saved the following letters and contracts to show what it was like in the '30's in the major leagues at contract time for me. It is interesting to contrast present salaries with these; although my contracts were quite satisfactory for the times. This was the time of the Great Depression. You may note that the letters often sound cautious, no one going out on a limb here.

It took a year before my last name was spelled correctly.

In the first three letters the monthly salary increased 125 dollars between January 12, 1931 and February 18, 1931.

The Detroit contract gives a flavor of the times in the fine print."

IMPORTANT NOTICE

The attention of both Club and Player is specifically directed to the following excerpt from Article II, Section 1, of the Major League Rules:

"No Club shall make a contract different from the uniform contract or a contract containing a non-reserve clause, except with the written approval of the Advisory Council. All contracts shall be in duplicate and the Player shall retain a counterpart original. The making of any agreement between a Club and Player not embodied in the contract shall subject both parties to discipline by the Commissioner."

American League of Professional Baseball Clubs
UNIFORM PLAYER'S CONTRACT

Parties   The .... Detroit Baseball Company ....,

herein called the Club, and............ Marvin Owens ....,

of .... San Jose, California ...., herein called the Player.

Recital   The club is a member of the American League of Professional Baseball Clubs. As such, and jointly with the other members of the League, it is a party to agreements and rules with the National League of Professional Baseball Clubs and its constituent clubs, and with the National Association of Professional Baseball Leagues. The purpose of these agreements and rules is to insure to the public wholesome and high-class professional baseball by defining the relations between Club and Player, between club and club, between league and league, and by vesting in a designated Commissioner broad powers of control and discipline, and of decision in case of disputes.

Agreement   In view of the facts above recited the parties agree as follows:

Employment   1. The Club hereby employs the Player to render skilled service as a baseball player in connection with all games of the Club during the year.. 193..1 .... including the Club's training season, the Club's exhibition games, the Club's playing season, and the World Series (or any other official series in which the Club may participate and in any receipts of which the player may be entitled to share); and the player covenants that he will perform with diligence and fidelity the service stated and such duties as may be required of him in such employment.

Salary   2. For the service aforesaid the Club will pay the Player an aggregate salary of $............ ...... $625.00 a month ...., as follows:

In semi-monthly installments after the commencement of the playing season covered by this contract, unless the Player is "abroad" with the Club for the purpose of playing games, in which event the amount then due shall be paid on the first week-day after the return "home" of the Club, the terms *"home"* and *"abroad"* meaning, respectively, *at* and *away from* the city in which the Club has its baseball field.

If a monthly salary is stipulated above, it shall begin with the commencement of the Club's playing season (or such subsequent date as the Player's services may commence) and end with the termination of the Club's scheduled playing season, and shall be payable in semi-monthly installments as above provided.

If the Player is in the service of the Club for part of the playing season only, he shall receive such proportion of the salary above mentioned, as the number of days of his actual employment bears to the number of days in the Club's playing season.

Loyalty   3. (a) The Player will faithfully serve the Club or any other Club to which, in conformity with the agreements above recited, this contract may be assigned, and pledges himself to the American public to conform to high standards of personal conduct, of fair play and good sportsmanship.

(b) The Player represents that he does not, directly or indirectly, own stock or have any financial interest in the ownership or earnings of any Major League club, except as hereinafter expressly set forth, and covenants that he will not hereafter, while connected with any Major League club, acquire or hold any such stock or interest except in accordance with Section 23 (e), Article II, Major League Rules.

Service   4. (a) The Player agrees that, while under contract or reservation, he will not play baseball (except post-season games as hereinafter stated) otherwise than for the Club or a Club assignee hereof; that he will not engage in professional boxing or wrestling; and that, except with the written consent of the Club or its assignee, he will not engage in any game or exhibition of football, basketball, hockey, or other athletic sport.

Post-season Games   (b) The Player agrees that, while under contract or reservation, he will not play in any post-season baseball games except in conformity with the Major League Rules; and that he will not play in any such baseball game after October 31st any year until the following training season, or in which more than two other players of the Club participate, or with or against any ineligible player or team.

Assignment   5. (a) In case of assignment of this contract to another Club, the Player shall promptly report to the assignee club within 72 hours from the date he receives written notice from the Club of such assignment, if not more than 1600 miles by most-direct available railroad route, plus an additional 24 hours for each additional 800 miles; accrued salary shall be payable when he so reports; and each successive assignee shall become liable to the Player for his salary during his term of service with such assignee, and the Club shall not

Marv's 1931 Contract with Detroit

DUPLICATE

(Form 1931)

AMERICAN LEAGUE
PLAYER'S CONTRACT

The_____

Detroit Baseball Company,
(Club)

Of Detroit, Michigan.
WITH

Marvin Owens
(Player)

Of San Jose, California.

Approved:

_____
President, American League of Professional Baseball Clubs

_____, 193___

be liable therefor. If the Player fails to report as above specified, he shall not be entitled to salary after the date he receives written notice of assignment. If the assignee is a member either of the National or American League, the salary shall be as above (paragraph 2) specified. If the assignee is any other Club the Player's salary shall be the same as that usually paid by said Club to other players of like ability.

Termination (b) This contract may be terminated at any time by the Club or by any assignee upon ten days' written notice to the Player.

Regulations 6. The Player accepts as part of this contract the Regulations printed on the third page hereof, and also such reasonable modifications of them and such other reasonable regulations as the Club may announce from time to time.

Agreements and Rules 7. (a) The Major and Major-Minor League Agreements and Rules, and all amendments thereto hereafter adopted, are hereby made a part of this contract, and the Club and Player agree to accept, abide by and comply with the same and all decisions of the Commissioner pursuant thereto.

Publication (b) It is further expressly agreed that, in consideration of the rights and interest of the public, the Club, the League President, and/or the Commissioner may make public the record of any inquiry, investigation or hearing held or conducted, including in such record all evidence or information given, received or obtained in connection therewith, and including further the findings and decisions therein and the reasons therefor.

Renewal 8. (a) On or before February 15th (or if Sunday, then the succeeding business day) of the year next following the last playing season covered by this contract, by written notice to the Player at his address following his signature hereto (or if none be given, then at his last address of record with the Club), the Club or any assignee hereof may renew this contract for the term of that year except that the salary shall be such as the parties may then agree upon, or in default of agreement the Player will accept such salary rate as the Club may fix, or else will not play baseball otherwise than for the Club or for an assignee hereof.

(b) The Club's right of reservation of the Player, and of renewal of this contract as aforesaid, and the promise of the Player not to play otherwise than with the Club or an assignee hereof, have been taken into consideration in determining the salary specified herein and the undertaking by the Club to pay said salary is the consideration for both said reservation, renewal option and promise, and the Player's service.

Disputes 9. In case of dispute between the Player and the Club or any Major League Club assignee hereof, the same shall be referred to the Commissioner as an umpire, and his decision shall be accepted by all parties as final; and the Club and the Player agree that any such dispute, or any claim or complaint by either party against the other, shall be presented to the Commissioner within one year from the date it arose.

Supplemental Agreements 10. The Club and Player covenant that this contract fully sets forth all understandings and agreements between them, and agree that no other understandings or agreements, whether heretofore or hereafter made, shall be valid, recognizable, or of any effect whatsoever, unless expressly set forth in a new or supplemental contract executed by the Player and the Club (acting by its president, or such other officer as shall have been thereunto duly authorized by the president or Board of Directors, in writing filed of record with the League President and Commissioner—and that no other Club officer or employe shall have any authority to represent or act for the Club in that respect), and complying with all agreements and rules to which this contract is subject.

Special Covenants
See
"Important
Notice"
above.

This contract shall not be valid or effective unless and until approved by the League President or Advisory Council, as the case may be.

Signed in duplicate this................17th................ day of ....February................, A. D. 193..1..

[SEAL]

Detroit Baseball Company,
(Club)

Witness:

By_____
(President)

_____
(Player)

_____
(Home address of Player)

DETROIT BASEBALL COMPANY

OFFICE AND GROUNDS NAVIN FIELD
MICHIGAN AND TRUMBALL AVES.
DETROIT, MICHIGAN

Jan. 12, 1931.

Dear Mr. Owens: (sic)

I am herewith enclosing a probationary contract calling for $500 a month, the same as you received last year. If you remain with our club after May 1, I will see that you are given a satisfactory increase. On receipt of signed contract at this office you will be forwarded duplicate of same.

What I have heard about you is very encouraging, but everyone is a little doubtful as to whether you are ready for the Major Leagues right now. However, that is something no one can tell about and it might be you will remain with us all year.

You no doubt are aware of the fact that we are going to train at Sacramento this year and you are expected to report there on March 1. You will be notified later as to transportation, etc.

Hoping you are having a good winter and with best wishes, I am,

Very truly yours,
Frank J. Navin
Registered

DETROIT BASEBALL COMPANY

OFFICE AND GROUNDS NAVIN FIELD
MICHIGAN AND TRUMBALL AVES.
DETROIT, MICHIGAN

Jan. 29, 1931.

Dear Mr. Owens: (sic)

Replying to yours of recent date, as a matter of fact you are entitled to an increase over your contract of last year, and I will give it to you if you so desire, but I thought it would be better to wait until the end of the training season and then Manager Harris could decide exactly whether he would want you to remain with the club or be placed out for another year on option.

We have heard very good reports regarding your ability but you no doubt fully realize you have had very little professional experience. If we send you out on option we will make the best contract terms we can for you with some Class AA club, and if you remain with our club you will get a reasonable increase over the $500 a month offered you; or if you want a straight contract calling for $625.00 a month, it will be sent to you. Please advise me as to what your decision is in the matter.

The transportation in your case is a very lucky break for us, but you must realize we have players coming from all over the country and our transportation expense is tremendous, especially when we go to the coast. The Major League clubs do not pay transportation home at the end of the season.

Wishing you every success, I am,
Very truly yours,
Frank J. Navin

DETROIT BASEBALL COMPANY

OFFICE AND GROUNDS NAVIN FIELD
MICHIGAN AND TRUMBALL AVES.
DETROIT, MICHIGAN

Feb. 18, 1931.

Dear Mr. Owens: (sic)

Replying to yours of the 13th, I herewith enclose contract calling for $625.00 a month which please sign and return to me. I am also enclosing duplicate for your reference.

Wishing you every success, I am,

Very truly yours,
Frank J. Navin

REGULATIONS

1. The Club's playing season for each year covered by this contract and all renewals hereof shall be as fixed by the American League of Professional Baseball Clubs, or if this contract shall be assigned to a Club in another league, then by the league of which such assignee is a member.

2. The Player must keep himself in first-class physical condition and must at all times conform his personal conduct to standards of good citizenship and good sportsmanship.

3. The Player, when requested by the Club, must submit to medical examination at the expense of the Club and, if necessary, to treatment by a regular physician in good standing at the Player's expense. Disability directly resulting from injury sustained in playing baseball for the Club while rendering service under this contract shall not impair the right of the Player to receive his full salary for the season in which the injury was sustained, but only upon the express prerequisite condition that written notice of such injury, including the time, place, cause and nature of the injury, is served upon and received by the Club within twenty days of the sustaining of said injury. Any other disability may be ground for suspending or terminating this contract at the discretion of the Club.

4. The Club will furnish the Player with two complete uniforms, exclusive of shoes, the Player making a deposit of $30.00 therefor, which deposit will be returned to him at the end of the season or upon the termination of this contract, upon the surrender of the uniforms by him to the Club.

5. The Club will provide and furnish the Player while "abroad," or traveling with the Club in other cities, with proper board, lodging, and pay all proper and necessary traveling expenses, including Pullman accommodations and meals en route.

6. For violation by the Player of any regulation the Club may impose a reasonable fine and deduct the amount thereof from the Player's salary or may suspend the Player without salary for a period not exceeding thirty days, or both, at the discretion of the Club. Written notice of the fine or suspension or both and of the reasons therefor shall in every case be given to the Player.

7. In order to enable the Player to fit himself for his duties under this contract, the Club may require the Player to report for practice at such places as the Club may designate and to participate in such exhibition contests as may be arranged by the Club for a period of .... 30 ....days prior to the playing season without any other compensation than that herein elsewhere provided, the Club, however, to pay the traveling expenses, including Pullman accommodations, and meals en route, of the Player from his home city to the training place of the Club, whether he be ordered to go there direct or by way of the home city of the Club. In the event of the failure of the Player to report for practice or to participate in the exhibition games, as provided for, he shall be required to get in playing condition to the satisfaction of the Club's team manager, and at the Player's own expense, before his salary shall commence.

DETROIT BASEBALL COMPANY

OFFICE AND GROUNDS NAVIN FIELD
MICHIGAN AND TRUMBALL AVES.
DETROIT, MICHIGAN

Feb. 9, 1932.

Dear Mr. Owen:

I have yours of the 5th. If you sign a contract with us for
$625.00 a month and you are sent out on option, I could
not reduce the amount in the original contract if I wanted
to. The rule is a player sent out on option has to receive
the salary the original contract called for. The other part
of the contract - that in the event of you staying with our
club and being worth more than $625.00 to us, you will
have to take my word for. If you do not feel that you will
be protected you can put this letter aside as a
memorandum of our arrangement.

I am enclosing herewith contract which please sign and
return; also duplicate of same for your reference.

Very truly yours,
Frank J. Navin

DETROIT BASEBALL COMPANY

OFFICE AND GROUNDS NAVIN FIELD
MICHIGAN AND TRUMBALL AVES.
DETROIT, MICHIGAN

Jan. 9, 1935.

Friend Owen:

I am enclosing contract for the season of 1935 calling for
$6000.00 This is about a 40 percent increase over what
you received last year, not considering the bonus given you
at the end of the year. This is the first good year you had
with us and I hope you can keep going. You looked pretty
tired at the end of the season last year, but I hope you will
come back all right this spring. On receipt of signed
contract at this office duplicate will be sent to you.

Later you will be advised to report at Lakeland on
March 10.

Hoping you are having a pleasant winter and with best
wishes for a successful season, I am,

Very truly yours,
Frank J. Navin
Registered
Receipt Requested

American League of Professional Baseball Clubs

UNIFORM PLAYER'S CONTRACT

Parties   The............**Detroit Baseball Company**............................

herein called the Club, and............**Marvin Owen**...............................

of............**San Jose, California.**............................, herein called the Player.

Recital   The Club is a member of the American League of Professional Baseball Clubs. As such, and jointly with the other members of the League, it is a party to the American League Constitution and to agreements and rules with the National League of Professional Baseball Clubs and its constituent clubs, and with the National Association of Professional Baseball Leagues. The purpose of these agreements and rules is to insure to the public wholesome and high-class professional baseball by defining the relations between Club and Player, between club and club, between league and league, and by vesting in a designated Commissioner broad powers of control and discipline, and of decision in case of disputes.

Agreement   In view of the facts above recited the parties agree as follows:

Employment   1. The Club hereby employs the Player to render skilled service as a baseball player in connection with all games of the Club during the year....193...6....including the Club's training season, the Club's exhibition games, the Club's playing season, and the World Series (or any other official series in which the Club may participate and in any receipts of which the player may be entitled to share); and the player covenants that he will perform with diligence and fidelity the service stated and such duties as may be required of him in such employment.

Salary   2. For the service aforesaid the Club will pay the Player an aggregate salary of $...............**$7000.00**............................., as follows:

In semi-monthly installments after the commencement of the playing season covered by this contract, unless the Player is "abroad" with the Club for the purpose of playing games, in which event the amount then due shall be paid on the first week-day after the return "home" of the Club, the terms "home" and "abroad" meaning, respectively, at and away from the city in which the Club has its baseball field.

If a monthly salary is stipulated above, it shall begin with the commencement of the Club's playing season (or such subsequent date as the Player's services may commence) and end with the termination of the Club's scheduled playing season, and shall be payable in semi-monthly installments as above provided.

If the Player is in the service of the Club for part of the playing season only, he shall receive such proportion of the salary above mentioned, as the number of days of his actual employment in the Club's playing season bears to the number of days in said season.

Loyalty   3. (a) The Player will faithfully serve the Club or any other Club to which, in conformity with the agreements above recited, this contract may be assigned, and pledges himself to the American public to conform to high standards of personal conduct, of fair play and good sportsmanship.

(b) The Player represents that he does not, directly or indirectly, own stock or have any financial interest in the ownership or earnings of any Major League club, except as hereinafter expressly set forth, and covenants that he will not hereafter, while connected with any Major League club, acquire or hold any such stock or interest except in accordance with Major League Rule 20 (e).

Service   4. (a) The Player agrees that, while under contract or reservation, he will not play baseball (except post-season games as hereinafter stated) otherwise than for the Club or a Club assignee hereof; that he will not engage in professional boxing or wrestling; and that, except with the written consent of the Club or its assignee, he will not engage in any game or exhibition of football, basketball, hockey or other athletic sport.

Post-season Games   (b) The Player agrees that, while under contract or reservation, he will not play in any post-season baseball games except in conformity with the Major League Rules; and that he will not play in any such baseball game more than ten days after the close of the Major League championship season any year covered by this contract, until the following training season, or in which more than two other players of the Club participate, or with or against any ineligible player or team.

Assignment   5. (a) In case of assignment of this contract to another Club, the Player shall promptly report to the assignee club within 72 hours from the date he receives written notice from the Club of such assignment, if not more than 1600 miles by most-direct available railroad route, plus an additional 24 hours for each additional 800 miles; accrued salary shall be payable when he so reports; and each successive assignee shall become liable to the Player for his salary during his term of service with such assignee, and the Club shall not

be liable therefor. If the Player fails to report as above specified, he shall not be entitled to salary after the date he receives written notice of assignment. If the assignee is a member either of the National or American League, the salary shall be as above (paragraph 2) specified. If the assignment, either outright or optional, is made to any other Club, then the Player's salary shall be the same as that usually paid by said Club to other players of similar ability in the same classification.

The foregoing shall apply not only in case of assignment of this contract to another club, but also when the transfer is to a club which the Club (party hereto) owns or controls. A subsequent retransfer by such subsidiary to the Club (party hereto) either the same season, or thereafter, shall not entitle the player to be paid any salary lost by the player as a result of such transfer or transfers.

Termination   (b) This contract may be terminated at any time by the Club or by any assignee upon ten days' written notice to the Player.

Regulations   6. The Player accepts as part of this contract the Regulations printed on the third page hereof, and also such reasonable modifications of them and such other reasonable regulations as the Club may announce from time to time.

Agreements and Rules   7. (a) The American League Constitution, and the Major and Major-Minor League Agreements and Rules, and all amendments thereto hereafter adopted, are hereby made a part of this contract, and the Club and Player agree to accept, abide by and comply with the same and all decisions of the Commissioner, and/or League President or Board of Directors, pursuant thereto.

Publication   (b) It is further expressly agreed that, in consideration of the rights and interest of the public, the Club, the League President, and/or the Commissioner may make public the record of any inquiry, investigation or hearing held or conducted, including in such record all evidence or information given, received or obtained in connection therewith, and including further the findings and decisions therein and the reasons therefor.

Renewal   8. (a) On or before February 15th (or if Sunday, then the succeeding business day) of the year next following the last playing season covered by this contract, by written notice to the Player at his address following his signature hereto (or if none be given, then at his last address of record with the Club), the Club or any assignee hereof may renew this contract for the term of that year except that the salary shall be such as the parties may then agree upon, or in default of agreement the Player will accept such salary rate as the Club may fix, or else will not play baseball otherwise than for the Club or for an assignee hereof.

(b) The Club's right of reservation of the Player, and of renewal of this contract as aforesaid, and the promise of the Player not to play otherwise than with the Club or an assignee hereof, have been taken into consideration in determining the salary specified herein and the undertaking by the Club to pay said salary is the consideration for both said reservation, renewal option and promise, and the Player's service.

Disputes   9. In case of dispute between the Player and the Club or any Major League Club assignee hereof, the same shall be referred to the Commissioner as an umpire, and his decision shall be accepted by all parties as final; and the Club and the Player agree that any such dispute, or any claim or complaint by either party against the other, shall be presented to the Commissioner within one year from the date it arose.

Supplemental Agreements   10. The Club and Player covenant that this contract fully sets forth all understandings and agreements between them, and agree that no other understandings or agreements, whether heretofore or hereafter made, shall be valid, recognizable, or of any effect whatsoever, unless expressly set forth in a new or supplemental contract executed by the Player and the Club (acting by its president, or such other officer as shall have been thereunto duly authorized by the president or Board of Directors, in writing filed of record with the League President and Commissioner—and that no other Club officer or employe shall have any authority to represent or act for the Club in that respect), and complying with all agreements and rules to which this contract is subject.

Special Covenants   See "Important Notice" above.

This contract shall not be valid or effective unless and until approved by the League President or Advisory Council, as the case may be.

Signed in duplicate this............**7th**............day of............**February**............, A. D. 193..**6**.
[SEAL]

........................**Detroit Baseball Company,**........................
(Club)

By..........**Walter O. Briggs**..........
(President)

Witness:...

....
(Player)

....
(Home address of Player)

Marv's 1936 Contract with Detroit

Detroit was the center of the automobile industry so most of the players purchased their cars from dealers in Detroit. Over the years, Marv purchased cars from Ford Co. and General Motors.

The bill of sale for a new deluxe 1935 Ford coupe details the cost of the car, federal and state tax, license and title, gas and oil and delivery charge.

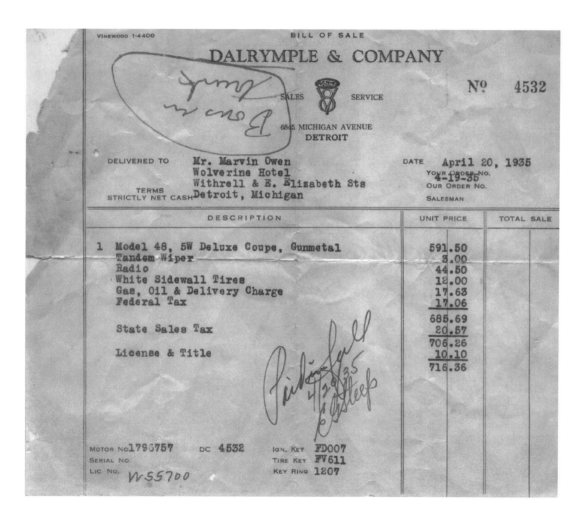

Marv shipped the car home and noted that the bonus was in the trunk. $716.36 was the cost of a new deluxe 1935 Ford coupe.

Homers & Cereal

What do baseball players receive in the 1990's as gifts for home runs they hit?
The following letter demonstrates what was given for hitting homers in the '30's.

DISTRIBUTORS OF
CORN FLAKES
PEP
ALL-BRAN
WHOLE WHEAT BISCUIT
WHEAT KRUMBLES
RICE KRISPIES
WHOLE WHEAT FLAKES
KAFFEE HAG COFFEE

PRODUCTS MANUFACTURED AT
BATTLE CREEK, MICHIGAN
LONDON, CANADA
SYDNEY, AUSTRALIA

1504 PAUL BROWN BLDG., ST. LOUIS, MO.

July 14, 1936.

Mr. Marvin Owen,
% American League Baseball Club,
Detroit, Michigan.

Dear Mr. Owen:

We are pleased to send you, under separate cover, a Sheaffer pen and pencil set, as the gift offered by the Kellogg Company for your first home run this year, at Sportsman's field. The reward for a second home run is a Sheaffer ladies' pen and pencil set, with any further home runs this year being rewarded with a special gift box, containing a supply of the individual size packages of the different Kellogg cereals.

The Kellogg Company is delighted to have the pleasure and privilege of having France Laux broadcast the St. Louis baseball games over station KMOX. We, too, assure you that we deeply appreciate the sincere cooperation of the ball clubs and players. We trust that our efforts will greatly further and cause a better understanding of the great sport in which you are engaged.

Whenever you, your family, or your friends are in the vicinity of Battle Creek, we hope you will accept this invitation to visit the "Home of Kellogg's"- the largest manufacturers of ready to eat cereals in the world.

With congratulations on your prize-winning wallop and with best wishes for a most successful season, we are

Sincerely,

KELLOGG SALES COMPANY

DISTRICT SALES MANAGER

RRA:L

DISTRIBUTORS
OF
CORN FLAKES
PEP
ALL-BRAN
WHOLE WHEAT BISCUIT
WHEAT KRUMBLES
RICE KRISPIES
WHOLE WHEAT FLAKES
KAFFEE HAG COFFEE

PRODUCTS MANUFACTURED
AT
BATTLE CREEK, MICHIGAN
LONDON, CANADA
SYDNEY, AUSTRALIA

1504 PAUL BROWN BLDG., ST. LOUIS, MO.

October 7, 1937.

Mr. Marvin Owen,
American League Baseball Club,
Detroit, Michigan.

Dear Mr. Owen:

We take great pleasure in attaching a $5.00 certificate good for $5.00 worth of groceries in any grocery store in the United States, or for merchandise at any of the stores listed on the reverse side.

The Kellogg Company is broadcasting the ball games in St. Louis over Station KMOX, and are offering these $5.00 certificates to any player hitting a home run, or to any pitcher pitching a five-hit ball game or less, or shut-out game at Sportsman's Park.

We trust that you will get as much fun spending this $5.00 as we do in presenting it to you. With kindest regards, I am

Yours very truly,

KELLOGG SALES COMPANY

DISTRICT SALES MANAGER

RRA:L

CHICAGO   NEW YORK

BLACKETT-SAMPLE-HUMMERT, INC.

ADVERTISING
221 NORTH LA SALLE STREET
CHICAGO,

October 22, 1938
Mr. Marvin Owen
362 South 6th Street
San Jose, California

Dear Mr. Owen:

Please find enclosed check for $150.00. This is in connection with the WHEATIES endorsement which you signed at the close of the baseball season this year.

Thank you very much for your cooperation in this matter. We hope that you are having a very swell vacation.

Very sincerely yours,

BLACKETT-SAMPLE-HUMMERT, Inc.

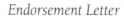

Endorsement Letter

An old penny postcard with baseball as a popular theme

Infield of Dreams
Greenberg, 1st base, Gehringer, 2nd base, Rogell, shortstop, and Owen 3rd base at Yankee Stadium, August 14, 1934
(Credit:Acme/Bettmann)

Infield of Dreams:

Elmer Kapp and Billy Rogell gave it this name because in 1934, the Tigers had one of the most productive infields in major league history. They had the most RBIs of any infield ever.

- The 1934 Tiger Infield of Hank Greenberg, 1st base, Charlie Gehringer, 2nd base, Billy Rogell, shortstop, and Marv Owen, 3rd base, amassed the greatest number of RBIs by an infield. Their total was 462 RBIs: Greenberg 139, Gehringer 127, Rogell 100 and Owen 96. In that same year Gehringer, Owen, Rogell each played all games that season, 154. Greenberg missed one game due to a Jewish holy day. The batting averages of the four players were: Greenberg .339, Gehringer .356, Rogell .296 and Owen .317. Each of the four 1934 infielders fielded over 950.

Their statistics:

PLAYER	POS	AVG	HR	RBI
Hank Greenberg	1B	.339	26	139
Charlie Gehringer	2B	.356	11	127
Billy Rogell	SS	.296	3	100
Marv Owen	3B	.317	8	96
TOTALS		**.327**	**48**	**462**

- In 1935 the same infield had 420 RBIs with Greenberg 178, Gehringer 108, Rogell 71 and Owen 71.
- In 1936 the Tigers had a team batting average of .300 and Gehringer, Al Simmons, Goslin and Owen had RBIs of over 100.

In 1984 Marv designed and ordered commemorative Louisville slugger bats that documented the details of the 1934 Greatest RBIs Infield and had one sent to each of the four members of that '34 infield.

THE GREATEST RBI INFIELD IN HISTORY

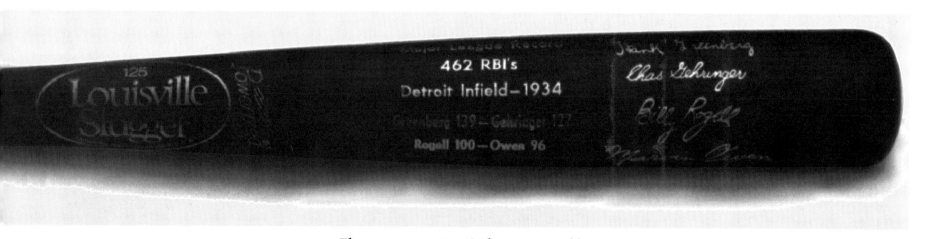

The commemorative '34 bat is pictured here.

The following excerpt is from a letter Marv received from Billy Rogell dated Nov. '84.

> 66 ..received the bat. Showed the bat to
> many people. They said it was great
> and so few people knew of our record.
> A sports writer from Tampa spent two
> hours with me about the 1934-35 ball
> club -- took pictures of the infield. He
> said how could anyone forget that
> infield. I was proud to be a member of
> that infield. Keep in touch. Again
> thanks for the bat -- great thought.
>
> As ever
> Bill Rogell
>
> P.S. I will be 80 on November 24.
> I'm an old goat. 99

The infield was like beauty in motion, though some called it, "The Battalion of Death."

Some baseball historians claim it was the best infield of all time. Detroit Tiger President Frank J. Navin said the infield was the greatest infield Detroit has had since he became connected with the club over thirty years ago.

August 25, 1935
In addition to having the most RBI (462) of any infield, the Tiger infield was rated the best in baseball at the time. The numbers in the picture indicate the number of errors of each player.
(Reprinted with permission of The Detroit News)

Rick Smith, General Manager of the Bakersfield Dodgers, in the #22, 1993 issue of the "Baseball Research Journal (SABR)" article, "Clutch Hitting or Good Fortune" offered the following chart.

Players with 100 or more RBIs
with a Slugging Percentage Below 400

Player/Team	G	AB	.AVG	2B	3B	HR	.SLG	RBI	Runs	CHI	BOP
B. Brubaker, '36 Pirates	145	554	.289	27	4	6	.384	102	804	160	6th
G. Wright, '27 Pirates	143	570	.281	26	4	9	.388	105	817	157	4th
M. Owen, '36 Tigers	154	583	.295	20	4	9	.389	105	921	137	7th
J. Carter '90 Padres	162	634	.232	27	1	24	.391	115	673	132	5th
H. Zimmerman, '17 Giants	150	585	.297	22	9	5	.391	102	635	171	4th
D. Pratt, '16 Browns	158	596	.267	35	12	5	.391	103	591	157	5th
B. Rogell, '34 Tigers	154	592	.296	32	8	3	.392	100	958	147	5th
W. Pipp, '23 Yankees	144	569	.304	18	8	6	.397	108	823	160	5th
R. Pepper, '34 Browns	148	564	.298	24	6	7	.399	101	674	140	4th

CHI = Clutch Hitting Index (see Total Baseball for full equation)   BOP = Batting Order Position   Compiled by Rick Smith

The following radio interview, July 4, 1934, of the Greatest RBI Infield demonstrates the mutual respect and regard of these four players.

(Reprinted with permission of The Detroit News.)

"GEHRINGER AT BAT" INTERVIEW

Wednesday, July 4th, 1934, 8:00 - 8:15 pm

ECCLES: Good evening, ladies and gentlemen. Once again the fighting Tigers are home – and here for a good long stay. They've just returned from one of the greatest road trips a Tiger team has ever made – with a fine win percentage – and firmly entrenched in second place, just a step from the leadership. And naturally, in welcoming the Tigers home we have the added pleasure of again having our own Charlie Gehringer with us. Now – just a word before we hear from Charlie. He never talks about himself and, therefore, someone has to talk about him. In the recent poll held to determine the players who will participate in the annual all-star game between the American and National Leagues, Gehringer received the greatest number of votes of any ball player for any position in the American League – and was second only to Bill Terry, that dynamic manager of the World's Champion New York Giants, in total votes cast by the baseball public. We believe this to be more significant than anything which might be said – as to just how much Charlie Gehringer means to baseball – and how firmly he has molded himself a place in the hearts of all sport loving people. We're happy to welcome Charlie Gehringer home.

(BRIDGE MUSIC — CLAP HANDS — HERE COMES CHARLIE OR "CHARLIE'S HOME" FADING INTO — GEHRINGER TALKING)

CHARLIE: Thank you, John. And thanks, Benny, for your swell greetings. We've been away so long – I almost feel like a stranger, like a visiting Rotarian or something.

ECCLES: Well, Charlie, we just finished giving the Rotarians a royal welcome to Detroit, and now that they've gone we can give all our time to you. After all, if the rest of the baseball world thinks so much of you, we ought to appreciate you that much more.

CHARLIE: All right. Now that the greetings are all over, I've got a real surprise for you.

ECCLES: What's that? **CHARLIE:** Wait just a moment. (SOUND OF DOOR OPENING) Come in, fellows. (SOUND OF DOOR CLOSING)
I want the radio public to meet three of the greatest fellows in the world — buddies of all of us. Hank Greenberg, Billy Rogell and Marvin Owen.

(BAND PLAYS "TIGER RAG")

ECCLES: Well, Charlie, this is sure a surprise, and a most pleasant one. And here, ladies and gentlemen, is the only .300 hitting infield in major league baseball. Henry Greenberg, first base. Charlie Gehringer, second base. Billy Rogell, short-stop, and Marvin Owen, third base. And while they're here, we might just as well put them to work on a few fast plays.

CHARLIE: Well, you pitch 'em, John, and we'll see how the boys bat in front of a mike.

ECCLES: O.K. Let's have Greenberg bat first. Hank, how do you like playing first base with the Tiger team?

GREENBERG: Fine, John. They're the best bunch of boys I've ever seen. And that goes both on and off the playing field.

ECCLES: Well, how does it feel playing first base with Gehringer, Rogell and Owen making up the rest of the infield?

GREENBERG: It's as easy as falling off a log. What I mean is that you can give all your attention to the play that's going on. You don't have to worry about what's going to happen and it helps a lot in keeping your own end up.

ECCLES: Just how do you mean?

GREENBERG: Well, suppose a ground ball is hit to my right. In a quick glance — I see that if I field it, I may not be able to get over to first fast enough for a play. So knowing that Gehringer is there, I'm pretty sure he'll get it, and I hoof it over to the bag ready for the ball and the put out. That's just one example.

ECCLES: Suppose you give us another.

GREENBERG: All right. A man's on second. We know the next play may be a bunt along first. It is. I come in to field it, knowing that if I can't make the play at third to get the runner going there, I can turn and throw to first and Gehringer will be there to take the ball for the out. He's the most perfect ball player I've ever seen, always doing the right thing, and making the hardest plays look easy.

ECCLES: O.K. Hank. That's two hits you've made on those first two pitches. Now watch this one— it's going to be a fast one. Why do you like to play with Owen and Rogell?

GREENBERG: That's easy, John. Because they're the greatest third baseman and short-stop in baseball. They're both ball hawks and once they get their hands on the ball — I know that all I have to do is reach out for it. Never a worry about a wild throw — digging it out of the dirt — or going into the air. They throw strikes on every play.

ECCLES: Well, Hank, that one was for extra bases. And now it's Billy Rogell's turn to bat.

ROGELL: Careful, John. I bat from either side of the plate.

ECCLES: Well, don't worry, Billy. These won't be left-handed throws. But seriously — you've been on a few clubs since your introduction to professional baseball — and it seems that not until the past couple of years have you really come into your own as a recognized first rater. How's that?

ROGELL: Well, that's sort of hard to answer, John. But I will say that I've never enjoyed playing ball as I have with the Tigers, especially since I've been teaming with Charlie Gehringer and the keystone sack.

ECCLES: Maybe that has something to do with it. You know they say that you never do so well until you really enjoy your work.

ROGELL: I suppose that's right — and that may be the answer.

ECCLES: Well, we hear so much about you or Charlie starting double plays — and both of you come up with impossible plays at the most crucial times — that maybe the inside story on that would be interesting.

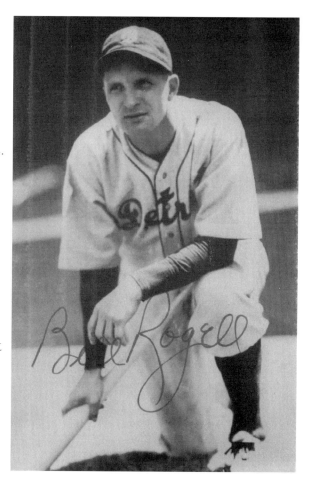

Billy Rogell, Shortstop
(*Thanks to: Bill Rogell*)

Charlie Gehringer
(Thanks to: Detroit Tigers)

ROGELL: I might say that in most cases it's almost automatic. After all, the double play is nothing more than perfect timing. You reach the bag at the same time that the ball gets there so that without any loss of time you can throw to first. When you don't have to worry about the second baseman's tosses as you're heading for that bag, it makes the rest of the play easy.

ECCLES: How does working with Gehringer affect your fielding?

ROGELL: It gives me greater freedom to work every possible angle of the shortstop position, because I know that if a ball is hit anywhere near second base, Charlie will get it if it's humanly possible to do so.

ECCLES: Well, how does Owen on the other flank affect your play?

ROGELL: Say, with Gehringer on one side and Owen on the other side of me, all I need is a davenport out at short stop to make my afternoon rest that much more comfortable.

ECCLES: And how does Greenberg fit into your picture?

ROGELL: Just look at the size of him. He'd fit into any picture. In fact, he'd be most of the picture. And that's just how it feels when you throw to first with Hank waiting for the ball. He's so big — and gets them from so many angles — up-down-wide — or wherever they come from, that you feel you can throw almost blind to first and he'll come up with the ball.

ECCLES: And I suppose that gives you the necessary ease of mind to let you concentrate on ground balls — and not worry so much about your throwing?

ROGELL: That's the point exactly.

ECCLES: Well, now that you and Greenberg have each batted a 1.000 let's turn to our other .300 batter, Marv — the first question which always comes to mind with respect to you is — have you gotten over that siege of sickness of last year?

OWEN: I'm sure glad to say that I'm all over it.

ECCLES: What was the matter? Do you mind telling us?:

OWEN: Not at all. The doctors say it was an idiosyncrasy.

ECCLES: What's that?

OWEN: A peculiar condition, something in my case like acute allergies. And every time I became over-heated I just broke out in a rash. And breathing was almost impossible.

ECCLES: And this year they've cured you completely, eh?

OWEN: Yes siree — and regardless as to how fast I move or how hot I get — I haven't had the least recurrence.

ECCLES: It's certainly great to hear that. And believe me, those of us who've watched you work at Navin Field all agree that you're the most improved player in baseball.

OWEN: Thanks, John, it's nice to be in good health again, but beyond that — working with Rogell, Gehringer and Greenberg can't help but bring up your game. You've heard about Gehringer and Greenberg tonight, but let me tell you that every time a ball is hit to me, I know that Rogell is right back of me to back me up. And that's a wonderful feeling. I've had a hard drive bounce off my glove only to have Rogell scoop it up and shoot it over to Hank for a put-out.

ECCLES: Well, how about your hitting?

OWEN: After all — you can't play with a bunch of fighting wild men without sort of getting the spirit. And when you've got a chap like Mickey Cochrane helping you correct your faults, and working with you, you can't help but come through.

ECCLES: Well, Marv — you, Rogell, and Greenberg have each hit a thousand at this mike tonight, and as for you, Charlie, I suppose you thought you'd get a spectator's seat tonight.

CHARLIE: Don't you think it's getting late, John? Benny looks as though he'd like to play a number.

ECCLES: Just one question, Charlie. How does it look to you for the next half of the season?

CHARLIE: Frankly, John, I think we're in good shape. We're right on the heels of New York in first place — with everybody in good physical condition. No injuries — pitching holding up — no great batting slumps — and above all the two greatest money players in baseball — Cochrane and Goslin.....

Hank Greenberg
(Thanks to: Detroit Tigers)

In 1933 an acute allergy plagued Marv whenever he would become too quickly overheated. In spring training he was often allowed to regulate his own schedule because he knew exactly how far he could push himself. If he exercised or trained too strenuously or too fast and became overheated, he would break out in a rash and his throat would swell making it extremely difficult to breathe. By working out in a very gradual manner in spring training, Marv could prepare himself carefully so that he could have a successful regular season.

This led to much speculation by the news reporters at spring training. "Will Marv Owen be playing at 3rd for Detroit this year?" The San Jose Evening News quoted the Detroit Evening Times "He has chased all pretenders away once again." "It is getting that every spring when Owen reports to the Tiger camp he finds a couple of phenoms threatening to take away his job. This spring was no exception, but again Owen's grip on the hot corner seems secure. He has shooed away all the pretenders."

Every year beginning in 1934 Marv and Tommie Bridges went to Hot Springs, Arkansas for the baths before they began spring training. Special consideration was given to Marv's physical conditioning. The following correspondence illustrates that fact.

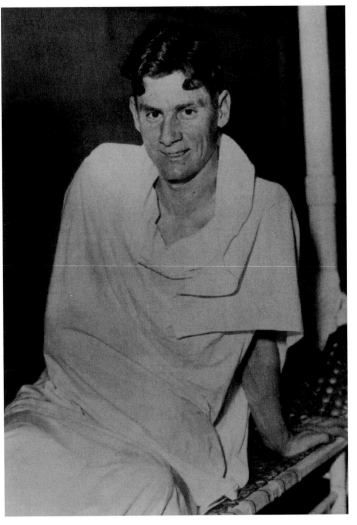

"Boiling Out"
(*World Wide Photos*)

58

DETROIT BASEBALL COMPANY

OFFICE AND GROUNDS NAVIN FIELD
MICHIGAN AND TRUMBALL AVES.
DETROIT, MICHIGAN

Dec. 28, 1934

Friend Marvin:

While there is no particular hurry, I just wrote to Tommie Bridges today suggesting that he go to Hot Springs before going to the training camp next year, because of the fact I think it did so much good for you last year. I suppose you would like to go back again this spring and I should like to have you go earlier than you did last year so you will be in camp when the rest of the fellows arrive there, and have a week or ten days' relaxation after the baths.

I hope you are having a good winter and that you will have a Happy and Successful New Year.

Very truly yours,
Frank J. Navin

DETROIT BASEBALL COMPANY

OFFICE AND GROUNDS NAVIN FIELD
MICHIGAN AND TRUMBALL AVES.
DETROIT, MICHIGAN

Jan. 12, 1935.

Friend Marvin:

Replying to yours of the 8th, I didn't know you had talked the matter over with Mike, but if he and you agreed on the time you are to report at the training camp, also the time you are to go to Hot Springs, it is all right with me. So I presume you will want to handle it the same as you did last year, that is, pay your own expenses and we will take care of it when you report at Lakeland.

With best wishes, I am,

Very truly yours,
Frank J. Navin

WESTERN UNION
1934 FEB 12 AM 9 45 FL47 36 DL=DETROIT MICH 12 1220P
MARVIN OWEN
#362 SOUTH SIXTH ST   SANJOSE CALIF
WIRE RECEIVED THINK YOUR SUGGESTION GOOD ONE MAKE YOUR OWN ARRANGEMENTS SUGGEST YOU LEAVE HOME AT
ONCE AND REMAIN AT HOTSPRINGS FOR AT LEAST THREE WEEKS OR LONGER IF NECESSARY DETROIT CLUB WILL PAY
YOUR EXPENSES   FRANK J NAVIN.

Bud Shaver wrote the following article at spring training in Lakeland, Florida.

Owen Never in Shape Until Season Opens

By Bud Shaver, Detroit Times

LAKELAND, Fla., March 16. --- Marvin Owen, the famous clinical case, is more puzzling than ever this Spring. Each year he staggers into training camp looking like a refugee from a wheel chair, dodders around until the gong rings and then he is in there making the fur fly.

The first Spring he reported at San Antonio, Tex., he had hay fever so bad that he blew all the top dressing off Neil Conway's infield with his sneezes.

Last Spring he arrived from Hot Springs, smelling of iodoform to face the cheerless prospect of being run off third base by healthier specimens.

Owen had a brief talk with Cochrane.

'Just let me train my own way,' he begged. **'I guarantee I'll be ready when the bell rings.'**

Clouts Line Drives

Cochrane agreed and Owen went through his meager training chores with the air and extreme care of a glass man doing a tap dance. When the bell rang, Owen was in there, banging out line drives and tossing base runners from third base into the visitors' dugout.

Everybody got in the habit of regarding Owen as a miracle of modern medical science, a complete and permanent cure.

But when Marvin Owen showed up this spring, several days late, he was the same old Owen. He tottered in with a hospital pallor, eyelids twitching and sniffling from a nose out of which surgeons had pried a couple of bones.

When he walked gingerly up to the plate the first time everyone held his breath, wondering if he'd make it. Without so much as spitting on his hands Owen belted a line drive into left field, walked slowly to the bench on his Leon Errol legs and sat down, a picture of utter exhaustion.

Comes to Life

That's his routine. He feels swell in the batter's box, but the slightest exertion around third base makes him positively ill.

If it was any one else you'd think it was a gag, but Owen is deadly serious about it. He has been doing it every Spring and the funny thing is that he seems to come to life as soon as the bell rings.

Heinie Schuble took Owen's infield practice every spring until Heinie's tongue hung out, but it was Owen's name which went in the box score when the season opened.

Spring training is just a waste of time to Owen. Frank J. Navin could save a lot of money and worry if he would just send Owen a railroad ticket with his contract and instructions:

'Be at Navin Field on opening day.'

(Reprinted with permission of The Detroit News)

It is interesting to note that Marv played every game in 1934 and 1936 (154 games each year).

Yet these were the words to describe
The Sick Man From San Jose:

- rifle-armed
- methodical
- quiet
- intelligent
- versatile, plays any infield position
- workmanlike
- covers plenty of territory
- sensational
- loose jointed
- accurate
- strong throwing arm
- magnificent
- marvelous
- veteran
- plays short hops better than any other 3rd baseman
- rangy
- steady
- handles 3rd with ease
- hard working
- keeps in good condition
- lean fellow.

But He Fooled 'Em

And then there is Marvin James Owen, the man from San Jose. He should surprise and please everybody. When the American League season ended last year, Owen was as dead as Lazarus in a baseball way. Ill all season, nobody thought he could make a comeback.

But Marvin has come back with a bang. In the spring training games he developed into what baseball knows as a sparkplug. He not only played his own position, third base, well, but also got so far over into shortstop territory that Billy Rogell had to beg him to let him into the ball game once in awhile.

For the first two weeks of the training season, Rogell, pop-eyed and mouth open in surprise, eyed Owen. Then he expressed his feelings.

"This Owen," he said, "he's got it. He's going to have a big year. He'll drive the fans dippy. Remember what I'm tellin' yuh."

Tigers Have Big Edge at Third

NEW YORK, Sept. 24—(A. P.)—Johnny Vergez, who is a pleasant young man but is having trouble keeping his batting average above .199, is causing Manager Bill Terry of the Giants many sleepless nights. Even Mr. Terry would trade Johnny to the Detroit Tigers for youthful Marvin Owen, and that seems to answer the question about who's who at the hot corner in the world series.

But the Giants won the world series last year without Vergez, who was out of the game with appendicitis. In his place then was Blondy Ryan, who made up in energy what he lacked in ability and played creditably through the classic.

It may be that Terry will use Ryan, again, and, if he does, Marvin Owen will still be the best third baseman in the series.

Six months ago Mickey Cochrane thought that the Tigers might possibly have a chance to finish on top of the American League, but it never occurred to him that twenty-five-year-old Owen would turn out to be just about the best third baseman in the league. The fact that he did has something to do with the Tigers' success.

In the spring, Cochrane tried to buy Pinkey Higgins from the Athletics, but Connie Mack was not interested in letting Higgins go to Detroit, so Mickey had to go along with Owen. Cochrane might even have put young Owen in a deal for

Higgins, and paid out good money into the bargain. He had no idea that Owen would bat over 70 points better than last year and that he would be slugging just as effectively as Higgins when the last month of the season rolled around. Still, Owen has done just that.

In addition to his hitting, Owen has had a great year in the field. He is not likely to cover more ground than Vergez, but he will throw more accurately and with more strength.

If Terry does decide to use Vergez, both third basemen will be starting in their first world series.

	G	AB	R	H	RBI	Pct
Owen	149	556	79	176	93	.317
Vergez	107	319	31	64	29	.201
Ryan	107	373	35	91	30	.244

The Detroit

WEATHER
Tuesday and
temperature.

Tuesday, September 25, 1934. 104th Year. No. 144

On Guar

TIGERS

READ THE GLADSOME DETAI

New Jersey Will Charge

Mother Think
Gallaher Chil

Free Press

ver a Century   26 Pages   Three Cents

FIN
EDITION

IN FLAG

PENNANT

TODAY'S SPORTS SECTION

usiness Demands Showdown

PENNANT FEVER

(Credit: Detroit Tigers)

The 1934 and 1935 Detroit Tigers were Detroit's first pennant contenders in two decades. They lost in 1934 and won in 1935. The 1934 Detroit Tigers–St. Louis Cardinals World Series may be remembered as one that Detroit lost and one that included the Medwick-Owen incident.

Here are the words of the songs distributed to the Detroit fans.

"FIGHT WITH THE FIGHTING TIGERS"
Lyrics by Anne Campbell
Music by Frank E. Wrigley

Let's drink a toast to the Tigers tonight,
We who are in their debt
You've taught us a goal can be won with a fight,
A lesson we'll not forget!

CHORUS:

Fight with the fighting Tigers!
Fight though the pennant's won!
Game by game, climb the hill to fame,
And your place in the sun!
Fight till the battle's over
And the Giants put to rout
We'll never give up, we'll never give up
Till the last man is out!

Let's drink a toast to the Tigers and say
"Thanks for a summer's fun!"
We'll tackle the troubles that crowd on our way
With thoughts of the goal you've won!

Tiger World Series Program 1934
(Thanks to Robert D. Opie)

64

AMERICAN LEAGUE PENNANT WINNERS, 1934

Detroit Tigers 1934
American League Pennant Winners
(Credit: National Baseball Library and Archive, Cooperstown, N.Y.)

Official Tiger Championship Ring

TIGERS ON PARADE
Lyrics by J. Fred Lawton
Music by Will E. Dulmage

Hear all the drumming, something is coming,
What can it be?
Hear all the cheering, something is nearing,
Oh gosh! Oh gee!
Here come the Tigers! Here come the Tigers!
Say can't you see the parade, the parade,
'Cause the Bengals made the grade.

CHORUS:

See the flags awavin' o'er the field of Navin
OH YOU TIGERS ON PARADE
Mickey's Aces have sure gone places,
Around those bases on parade.
COCHRANE! COCHRANE! What a man you are!
What a team and ev'ry man a star!
So all the world we're telling,
Ev'ry fan is yelling
OH YOU TIGERS ON PARADE.

Every Detroit Tiger owns a GRUNOW
(ad from back cover of 1934 program,
thanks to Robert D. Opie)

THE TIGER TEAM SONG
Lyrics by Pat Firzpatrick
Music by Fred Kahn and Wm. J. Turner

The Tiger team with lots of steam
Is bringing Detroit fame,
The pennant flag is in the bag,
There goes the old ball game,
With Mickey riled, the Tigers wild
Are pretty hard to tame,
Mister Navin, Flags are wavin'
One for every name!

CHORUS:

There's Bridges and Sorrell,
There's Baker and Rogell,
Hayworth, Hogsett, Fox and Hamlin,
Greenberg, Gehringer and Goslin,
Marberry and Owen,
Perkins, Doljack, Rowe an'
Fischer, Crowder, Auker, Walker, White,
Clifton, Carroll, Schuble too,
Mickey Cochrane we love you,
You've brought the pennant back to old Detroit!

Will Rogers and Mrs. Mickey Cochrane, October 1934
(credit: Detroit Free Press)

"TAKE ME OUT TO THE BALL GAME"

Take me out to the ball game,
Take me out to the park;
Buy me some peanuts and crackerjack
And I won't care if I never come back,
For it's root, root, root for the Tigers,
If they don't win it's a shame,
And it's one, two, three strikes, you're out!
At the old ball game.

THE 1934 WORLD SERIES- DETROIT TIGERS VS THE ST. LOUIS CARDINALS

Dizzy Dean and Schoolboy Rowe
(Detroit Free Press)

What factors contributed to the Tigers becoming the 1934 American League Champions for the first time in 25 years? A major factor was the baseball genius of Mickey Cochrane, catcher/manager, who was an inspiring leader with a fighting spirit. In addition, his hitting and catching skills were first class. As a catcher/manager he was able to work with newcomers; he was especially adept at developing the skills of pitchers, such as Tommy Bridges and Schoolboy Rowe.

The 1934 Tiger team was a balance of seasoned veterans and talented, eager youngsters. Together the veterans and the youngsters made a great blend of pitchers, fielders and hitters; the pitchers were: Auker, Bridges, Crowder, Hogsett, Marberry and Rowe. The infield of Greenberg, Gehringer, Rogell and Owen were called, "The Battalion of Death" and later, "The Infield of Dreams." Fox, Goslin, Walker, White and Doljack handled the field. The team had seven, steady .300 hitters and the whole team had great durability game after game. Three of the infielders played every game (154) of the 1934 season. The 4th infielder missed one game due to a religious holiday.

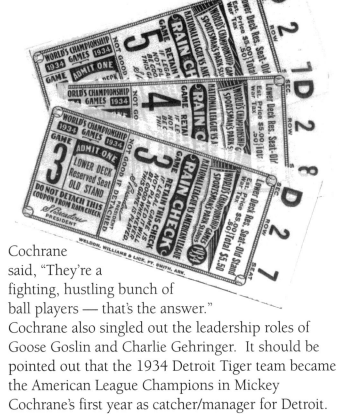

Cochrane said, "They're a fighting, hustling bunch of ball players — that's the answer." Cochrane also singled out the leadership roles of Goose Goslin and Charlie Gehringer. It should be pointed out that the 1934 Detroit Tiger team became the American League Champions in Mickey Cochrane's first year as catcher/manager for Detroit.

The rival St. Louis Cardinals, also known as "The Gashouse Gang", had winning pitchers in Dizzy and Paul Dean. Between the two of them pitching, the Cardinals won four games out of seven. The two brothers set an unequaled record.

Game	Score	Winning Pitcher
1	8-3	Dizzy Dean, St. Louis
2	3-2	Rowe, Detroit
3	4-1	Paul Dean, St Louis
4	10-4	Auker, Detroit
5	3-1	Bridges, Detroit
6	4-3	Paul Dean, St Louis
7	11-0	Dizzy Dean, St Louis

The Dean brothers were amazing!

Summing up the team's success, Manager Mickey

Hal Rhyne in reporting on the ill feeling of the 1934 Series wrote, "Detroit players felt that the Cards were sliding with their spikes too high and there has been a series of collisions and consequent ill-feeling between the players."

Pictured in the local papers were photos of the Detroit players surrounding Manager Cochrane after he had been spiked at first base in Monday's game. Another picture shows Medwick starting to slide into home plate, but Mickey blocks the plate and tags him out on a fine throw from Goslin. Beneath the action shot was "Cochrane was spiked on the play". This was game 2 in the 3rd inning. All of this may have played a part in the Owen/Medwick incident in the 6th inning of the seventh, final game.

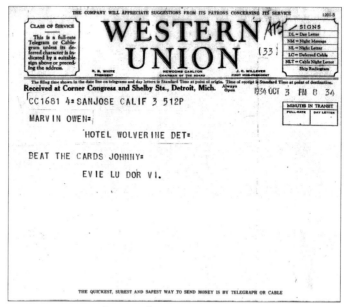

Telegram from Marv's sisters.

A fan wrote these words to be sung with a popular tune of the time. She sent them to Marv the day before the 1934 World Series began.

Freckle Face

Freckle Face, The very best third baseman 'round the place And in the game of baseball you're an ace. Your wonderful, Funny ol' Freckle Face. Freckle Face, You never flinch or bat an eye, When spikes of enemies come riding high. You never miss, Funny ol' Freckle Face. 'Twas not so long ago, about a year or so, That you were playing quite below par, But this year, you are swell, like a bat out of hell. You're fast and accurate, a shining star. Freckle Face, you've so much color and athletic grace. No other third baseman could e'er replace, Your winning plays, funny old Freckle Face.

Miss A_____ D_____

Owen/Medwick Incident
1934 World Series
(Credit:UPI/Bettmann)

You have probably heard of the Medwick-Owen incident. It happened in the 7th game of the 1934 World Series when Medwick of the Cardinals slid into third, where Tiger third sacker Owen was waiting. The newspaper accounts, the films and the discussions only raise questions. Where was the ball hit? Who threw it to third? Did Owen have the ball? Was there any bodily contact between Medwick and Owen? The questions go on. Even Detroit Tiger owner Frank J. Navin wrote to ask exactly what happened. When the side was retired and Medwick returned to his position in the outfield, he was pelted with fruit, vegetables and anything else that was handy. At any rate, Baseball Commissioner Judge Kenesaw Mountain Landis sensing the hostility of the fans, held court by talking to the principals. After discussion, he ruled that Medwick should leave the game so that order could be restored.

Marv did not like to talk about the incident but one thing he did say: "The concession man made a fortune selling stuff to throw out onto the field. He was a smart cookie." Charlie Gehringer wondered where the concessionaires got all the stuff to sell.

After the game was over, Marv was getting dressed in the locker room. Sitting on a bench and feeling grumpy after losing the game to the Cardinals, Marv was interrupted by a visit from Will Rogers who was probably the most popular public figure of the time. Will asked Marv, "What happened out there between you and Medwick?" Marv replied, "I don't want to talk about it." "That's the best advice I could give you, young man; you just stick with it."

Rehashing the Owen/Medwick Incident — What They Said:

John Lardner - "In the 6th inning, Joe hit the right field wall for three bases. Coming into third, he kicked his spikes at Detroit's Marv Owen, who had almost stepped on him."

Joe Cashman - "The next inning by way of retaliation, Medwick, in sliding into third did his level best to sever Owen's two legs from the rest of his frame."

Joe Falls, The Detroit Tigers - an Illustrated History - "The men bumped each other and stood nose to nose at the bag. Medwick was mad because Owen had duped him into thinking he had the ball, forcing Medwick to slide. Owen was irate because Medwick's spikes had nicked him on the slide."

Arthur Mann, Branch Rickey - "Medwick retaliated from a kneeing and had to be pulled from the flying fists of the third baseman."

William M. Anderson, The Detroit Tigers - "Cardinal Joe Medwick slides hard into third base and Marv Owen in the final game of the 1934 World Series, unleashing a Tiger fan furor."

Douglas Wallope, Baseball, A History - "Medwick spiked Owen."

Richard M. Cohen, David S. Neff, The World Series, Collier Books, Macmillan Co., 1986 - "With Dean pitching superbly, the Cards ran the score up to 9-0 when Joe Medwick slid hard into 3rd base and briefly wrestled with Tiger 3rd baseman Marv Owen."

Donald Honig, Baseball in the '30's, "Joe's slide into third was deemed overly aggressive by Marv Owen and a near-altercation took place between Joe and the Tiger third baseman."

Frankie Frisch, the Cardinal Manager - "Marv Owen got the ball and stepped on Medwick's leg. Joe kicked up from his position on his back and hit Owen in the chest. They started to fight and both teams boiled out."

H. G. Salsinger, Detroit News - "Umpire 'Beans' Reardon, whose testimony was solicited, says that to the best of his recollection, Owen took the throw but too late to tag Medwick. Others say the ball was cut off by Rogell and that Owen did not handle it."

Joe E. Brown, the late stage and screen comedian, in speaking about the 1934 incident, said he had the pictures to prove that Bill Rogell cut off the throw from the outfield and that Owen did not have the ball.

This is what **Iffy the Dopester** had to say, "Besides what did Joe Medwick do to us? He just jabbed his spikes right into the shins of our dearly beloved old Ham Hands, Marvin Owen. Just because he, playing third for us, lifted Joe's foot off the bag - nice as you please - and tagged him out as he came sliding in."

Will Rogers wrote in a letter to the editor of the Detroit Times: "I believe I am the only fellow who talked with both boys in their dressing rooms directly after the game. Medwick, whom I already knew, is a fine boy. And he felt very sorry, said it was just in the excitement of the game and he did it before he realized what he was doing, and that he had no hard feelings at all toward Owen. Owen was rightly nice about it. And said there was no attempt at a fight or argument and that he thought that Medwick had done what he did in the excitement."

Here is an excerpt from an October 9, 1934, Associated Press report that quotes **Commissioner Keneshaw Mountain Landis**:

"The 17,000 occupants of the left field bleachers were expressing their resentment for what they apparently believed was an attempt by Medwick to spike Marvin Owen, Tiger infielder, as he slid into third after tripling. Others considered the incident as just an exchange between the two players.

SAW WHAT HAPPENED.
'I saw what Medwick did and I couldn't blame the crowd for what it did,' was the comment after the game, of Commissioner Landis who took the unprecedented action of ordering Medwick from the game after taking statements from both the Cardinal outfielder and the Tiger third baseman at his box.'

'The bleacher crowd at the time was throwing debris upon the field as rapidly as groundkeepers could remove it, obviously determined that Medwick should not stay in the game.'

'The umpires in a World Series', Commissioner Landis continued. 'are instructed not to bench a player except for the most extreme cause, and so it was up to me. I did the proper thing."

OWEN SILENT. Medwick, who was escorted by six policemen to the Cardinal dressing room, said of the incident at third base: "I don't know what happened or how it happened. I just slid into third base, that's all.'

Owen refused to discuss it, except to say he was sorry Medwick had to leave the game."

Owen/Medwick Incident 1934 World Series
(National Baseball Library & Archive, Cooperstown, N.Y.)

Here is what some of the Detroit Tiger players thought months after the incident.

- Marv thought he had received the ball.
- Rogell thought he (Rogell) cut off the throw from the outfield. He thought Owen was in foul territory by 3rd base. Medwick slid into 3rd. So as not to step on Medwick, Owen fell on him and Medwick took offense.
- Tommy Bridges insisted that Marv caught the ball in the infield.
- Mickey Cochrane, Del Baker, Vic Sorrell, Gerald Walker, Elon Hogsett said Owen received the ball at third.
- Schoolboy Rowe, Ray Hayworth, Dennis Carroll, Fred Marberry and Hank Greenberg said Owen did not receive the ball.

Months after the incident, fans responding to the newspaper, voted 3 to 1 that Owen did not receive the throw.

A fan wrote to Marv:
"Mr. Owen, would you PLEASE tell me in writing about the famous incident you encountered with Joe Medwick in the 1934 Series?"

In 1983 Marv wrote to Jim Campbell, President of the Tigers, to see if he had any information regarding the incident. (He had no information.)

In 1986 Marv wrote to Peter V. Ueberroth, Baseball Commissioner, to see if any films could clarify the play. (No information.)

What were the questions?

- Who got the ball when it was returned to the infield?
- Did Owen have the ball when Medwick slid into third base?
- Did Owen receive the ball after Medwick slid into third?
- If the ball was thrown to Owen, who threw it?
- If Owen did not have the ball, why did Medwick slide?
- Who told him to slide?
- What happened when Medwick went into the bag?
- Are there any films that show definitely what happened?
- What REALLY happened is still the question today.

Here is Tiger Owner Frank J. Navin's letter requesting information regarding the incident.

DETROIT BASEBALL COMPANY
OFFICE AND GROUNDS NAVIN FIELD
MICHIGAN AND TRUMBULL AVES.
DETROIT, MICHIGAN

October 25, 1934.

Mr. Marvin J. Owen,
362 So. 6th Street,
San Jose, California.

Friend Marvin:

You told me something, before you went away, about the incident between you and Medwick. I wish you would write me and give me exactly what occurred to the best of your knowledge, for my own information. Another thing, I will be in a better position to answer in case I am asked about it by Judge Landis, who has no disposition to reopen the incident at all. He might ask me at the meeting exactly what occurred, for his own knowledge, and if I could not tell him, he might think I was evading the question.

The baseball people themselves want to know the exact truth on matters of this kind; therefore, I am writing you this letter, and you need not have any fear regarding the facts being made public. I am sure we all want the public to forget the affair, and we will not do anything to bring it up again.

Hoping that you will have a good winter, and with best wishes, I am

Very truly yours,

Frank J. Navin

FJN:LG

Here is the Chuck Hildebrand, Palo Alto Times, column of the fall of 1984.

"IT WAS A HARD LIFE in a lot of ways, but the years have treated Owen well. His eyes remain probing and alert, his posture unstooped, his voice firm and his memory clear. Around the athletic offices at Santa Clara, he is a frequent and welcome visitor–partly because he is a colorful storyteller, but also because he offers sound, contemporary advice. He is, in short, a good-natured, friendly and enjoyable individual–hardly the sort of person one would expect to be a central figure, albeit a reluctant one, in one of the ugliest scenes in World Series history.

But he was, and he knows with the 50th anniversary of the famous 1934 World Series coming up, the events of Oct. 9, 1934, will be debated anew.

What really happened between Owen and Joe Medwick of the St. Louis Cardinals that day?

'IT DOESN'T BOTHER ME to be remembered for that,' Owen said, 'but I know I'll be asked. It happened last June when I was invited back to Detroit for the ceremony when they retired the numbers of Hank Greenberg and Charlie Gehringer. A TV guy asked me about it when I was sitting in the dugout.

'The thing is, I never talked about it when Medwick was alive (he died in 1975), and I can't now. I would like people to know my side, but there would be so many people who would say I was gutless because I didn't talk when Medwick was alive.'

The prelude to the incident of Oct. 9, 1934, at Detroit's Briggs Stadium went something like this:

It was the sixth inning of the seventh game, and the Cardinals–known as the Gas House Gang because of their no-holds-barred style of play–led, 7-0. The Cardinals' Dizzy Dean was pitching with such defiant dominance that the outcome really wasn't in doubt, and the Tigers and most of the 40,902 fans unsurprisingly were in an ugly mood.

THE EXPLOSION CAME in the sixth inning, when Medwick, the Cardinals' left fielder, tripled. He barely beat the tag by Owen, who was playing third base, and the two collided on the play. Some say Medwick slid in with the intention of spiking Owen; others say it was a shove by Owen that started the altercation. In any case, a fight ensued.

When Medwick returned to his position, the fans, as the account puts it, 'bombarded him with overripe fruit, vegetables, lunch boxes and newspapers. (Commissioner Kenesaw Mountain) Landis removed Medwick to stop the disturbance.'

It is believed the only time in baseball history a player was ejected from a game–much less a World Series game– by a commissioner.

If anything, Owen finds the aftermath of the controversy somewhat amusing. 'I remember one time I saw a book in a library at Santa Clara,' he said. 'It was a history book on the World Series, so naturally I turned to the 1934 World Series. I read what it said, and I said to myself, 'Holy mackerel, I must have been in Chicago or someplace when that happened.' That sure wasn't the way I saw it.

'He (Medwick) was a rough guy, but a fine ballplayer, I'll say that. About half the people who saw it seemed to think I was wrong, and the other half say I was right. But the funny thing about it is the fact there are so many different versions of what happened.

'But no, I don't feel bitter about anything. I enjoyed baseball, and it was good to me. The only thing I regret is that I can't tell my side of the story.'
Better, in this case, to keep the distance."

October 1989 in an interview with Dave Anderson of the New York Times Owen said "Medwick slid extra hard into me at third base." "When he did that, I kicked him in the groin and he didn't like that."

When asked about losing the 1934 World Series in the 7th game at Detroit, Marv expressed it this way. "I didn't think of it as the end of the world. We knew we had a good ball club and lots of times in the World Series the breaks go your way and you win; the breaks don't go your way and you lose. With the play at third base, the man was out; I mean the man really was safe and the umpire called him out. He was one of our runners; that decided the game, the series for us. That's not alibiing. But, we knew we had a good ball club. We came back in 1935 and we won the World Series against the Cubs – four out of six. So everything turned out all right."

It is sad to think Marv is often remembered for the one incident, Medwick/Owen, than for all the other skills and talents he brought to the game. This columnist said it well:

In June 1934, H.G. Salsinger wrote, "In the current voting, inaugurated to select all-star American and National League Teams for the annual inter-league game at the Polo Grounds on July 18, several players are being well overlooked and none more completely than Marvin Owen, Detroit's third baseman.

Owen is not only the most improved ball player in the majors, but on what he has shown to date, he is the best third baseman in the league, the best fielder of them all and an extremely dangerous batter when there are men on bases. He will probably drive in more runs this year than any other third sacker." (He did.)

MARVIN OWEN—They call him Merv but his name is Marvin and he belongs to the California Owen family. There is no "s" attached to the family name but he never frets when reporters insist upon adding the "s." He won a pennant and "little world series" for Newark in 1932 but he showed little with Detroit last year because he was ill. They wanted to get another third baseman this spring but failed and so they had to use Owen. That was lucky for Detroit. He is probably the best third baseman in the league this year. A great fielder, he has the most powerful hands found on any American League infield, and the largest. He can hold seven baseballs in either hand. He is one of the team's best hitters and a very dangerous gent when there are men on bases. Hitting safely with the bases jammed is his specialty. He has a magnificent throwing arm and plays short hops better than any other third baseman.

(Credit: Detroit Tigers)

1935 World Series
Detroit Tigers vs Chicago Cubs
(Credit: National Baseball Library and Archive, Cooperstown, N.Y.)

The 1935 Detroit Tiger—Chicago Cubs Series may be best remembered because the Detroit Tigers were the winners!

Detroit won the 1935 World Series defeating the Chicago Cubs in six games. For Marv it was good news because the Tigers won the Series and because Marv had very successfully replaced injured Hank Greenberg at 1st base. The bad news was that Marv had gone 0–12 in the 1934 World Series and then went 0–19 in the 1935 World Series. The great good news was he singled to left off Larry French in the sixth, final game of the 1935 Series scoring Rogell to tie the score! He proved his worth when he got an intentional walk in the 8th inning of that game.

Whenever Marv was asked, "What was your greatest thrill playing with the Tigers?" He honestly replied, "Every game I played with them." One in particular he remembered. It was the 1935 World Series and he had gone to bat 19 times straight without a hit, 0 for 19. So here he was going up for the twentieth time. He said to himself everything I do is wrong – nothing right happens. So he decided no matter where the pitcher throws the ball, if he throws it ten feet above his head, he's going to swing. He threw it right down the middle of the plate. He got a line drive base hit to left center for his first hit that tied the score in the final game of the World Series. That was his biggest thrill and winning the World Series!

©1995 Ripley Entertainment Inc.
Registered Trademark of Ripley Entertainment Inc.

IFFY THE DOPESTER
(Credit: Detroit Free Press)

Here's what Iffy the Dopester of the Detroit Free Press had to say about that:

"Iffy...the Dopester rises to remark...

This, O my hearties, is the history of a man who found himself.

It is a tale which, if told well enough, would delight the mind of Matthew Arnold who caught a gleam of it when he wrote those beautiful lines:

Once read thy own breast right,
And thou hast done with fears!
Man gets no other light,
Search he a thousand years.

Mickey Cochrane
(Credit:: The Detroit News)

1935 *Tiger Souvenir Edition*

DETROIT TIMES

Only Detroit Newspaper Carrying International News — SUNDAY — Universal Service and Complete Sport Dispatches

35TH YEAR, NO. 343 — DETROIT, MICHIGAN, SUNDAY SEPTEMBER 8, 1935 — PRICE TEN CENTS

Iffy the Dopester continues:

Marvin Owen is the hero of the piece. All the expert experters have proclaimed him. He has been hitting better this spring than he ever has in his career. Home runs, doubles, singles. And hitting in the clutch. It is said about him that he went home to San Jose, Calif., last fall in the realization that he had a fight on his hands to remain on the team. It is further told that he spent the whole winter getting into physical shape for the fight to hold his job. That he triumphed.

Shucks!

That ain't the tale, Ladies and Gemmen. To understand the come-back of Marvin we must deal in metaphysics, with the intangible things of the spirit. He found himself. "Nothing can bring you peace but yourself," said Emerson in his classic essay on Self-Reliance, and Marv' found that inward peace in the greatest moment of his despair; that one awful agonizing second in the World Series of 1935 — when the championship depended upon him, and he came through.

All last summer Marv' seemed to be kind of feeling sorry for himself. On a warm August day he would be wearing a light overcoat with the collar turned up. He never complained, never talked about his troubles. Marv' is one of the quietest and best behaved and most intelligent young men in baseball. Some have paid him the doubtful compliment (for the others) of being so intelligent to be a good ballplayer. They mean by that that his intellectual outlook is higher than that of merely playing games. They get this suspicion because he does not roar and rant...

Iffy continues:

Only his marvelous defensive play kept him in the line-up through the latter part of last season. And yet the records show, surprisingly, that while his batting percentage was not so hot, the few hits he did get brought in a good many more runs than would be expected. He seemed to arouse himself in the pinches. While he only made 127 hits in 483 times at bat, he drove in 71 runs. Buddy Meyer, league champion hitter, made 215 hits but brought in 100 runs — in 616 times at bat.

Then came the World Series. Not anything that looked like a hit in that first game. Nor the second. And Hank Greenberg went out with his broken wrist. Opening in Chicago Marv' was told he had to play first base — his old position in the minors.

He took the job, struggling along with Hank's big mitt, but he was the least nervous man among the Tigers...

On the night after the last game in Chicago Old Iffy saw Marv' in the lobby of the hotel. His brow was even more corrugated than usual.

"Iffy," he said, "has any regular player ever gone through a whole World Series without making a hit?"

I told him I could not recall off-hand and asked him why he popped the question.

"Because," he said dolefully, "it looks as though if no such record ever has been made, I'm going to be the goat that will set it."

"You sure will be," I said, "as long as you are so positive that you are."

He grinned wryly and went his way.

Still no hits! And then came the last thrill-packed game of the series. The first time at bat in the last game French struck him out with three pitched balls. In the fourth with Walker and Rogell on, Manager Mike sent him in to sacrifice, but he could not even do that, forcing Fireman Bill at second.

The sixth inning came as sixth innings will. The Tigers one run behind. With two down Rogell slashed out a double. A groan came from the packed stands as Marv' Owen, the hitless wonder came up to the plate. Nineteen straight times in the series he had marched back with nary the semblance of a sock.

At that very moment with 40,000 pairs of eyes looking down upon him something happened inside Marvin Owen. He saw stretching before him the road to the end. His baseball career was over. No longer would he hear the roar of the crowds. His day was done. Now he would start on the career he had planned all his life — that of a school teacher. The strain of battle was over. He actually relaxed.

This, then, was his last appearance, his exit.

Perfectly cool, at ease with himself for the first time, he ceased to press. Calmly he walked to the plate and swung on the first ball pitched. His timing was perfect. The ball went on a line over short—a perfect hit. Billy Rogell came racing over the plate with the tying run. The world's Championship had been saved! The ninth inning finish is all too vivid history to be recalled now. But it was Marv's hit that made the glorious ending possible.

After the game that night Marvin was still the quiet scholarly gentleman. "I knew," he said, "the second I hit that ball, that I had conquered myself. I was cured. Never again will I get tense and tighten up at the plate. My fussing days are gone forever."

Iffy continues—

LYNWOOD "SCHOOLBOY"
ROWE
(Credit:National Baseball Library and Archive, Cooperstown, N.Y.)

Box Score of Title Game

CHICAGO

	AB	R	H	O	A	E
Galan, lf	4	0	1	2	0	0
Herman, 2b	4	1	3	3	4	0
Klein, rf	4	0	1	0	0	0
Hartnett, c	4	0	2	9	1	0
Demaree, cf	4	0	0	0	0	0
Cavarretta, 1b	4	0	1	8	1	0
Hack, 3b	4	0	2	0	4	0
Jurges, ss	4	1	1	3	2	0
French, p	4	1	1	1	2	0
Totals	37	3	12	x26	14	0

DETROIT

	AB	R	H	O	A	E
Clifton, 3b	5	0	0	2	0	0
Cochrane, c	5	2	3	7	0	0
Gehringer, 2b	5	0	2	0	4	0
Goslin, lf	5	0	1	2	0	0
Fox, rf	4	0	2	3	1	1
Walker, cf	2	1	1	0	0	0
Rogell, ss	4	1	2	2	3	0
Owen, 1b	3	0	1	11	0	0
Bridges, p	4	0	0	0	3	0
Totals	37	4	12	27	11	1

xTwo out when winning run was scored.

Chicago ....0 0 1 0 2 0 0 0 0—3
Detroit ....1 0 0 1 0 1 0 0 1—4

Runs batted in—Herman 3, Goslin 1, Fox 1, Owen 1, Bridges 1. Two-base hits—Fox, Gehringer, Rogell, Hack. Three-base hit—Hack. Home run—Herman. Sacrifice hit—Walker. Left on bases—Detroit 10, Chicago 7. Double play—Gehringer to Rogell to Owen. Bases on balls—Off French 2 (Walker, Owen). Struck out—By Bridges 7 (French 2, Hartnett, Demaree, Galan, Jurges, Cavarretta); by French 7 (Clifton 2, Bridges 2, Owen, Cochrane, Rogell). Umpires—Quigley (N), plate; McGowan (A), first; Stark (N), second; Moriarty (A), third.

Iffy continues—

As Old Iffy told you in the spring time when all the expert experters were picking various young men who were sure to take Owen's place, he'd be back on his old job at the hot corner. He is. And he made almost as many home runs in two days last week as he did all the season of 1935. Marvin Owen went through the Gethsemane of despair and found himself.

But he remains the same, imperturbable. At the victory baseball banquet Pete Fox refused to make a speech, though he led both teams by hitting .385. After his refusal they called on Owen.

'When a man who tops the World Series batters with .425 refuses to make a speech', said Marvin, 'what right have I—who batted .050?' And sat down. But that .050 was enough to save the series and to give Marvin a rebirth of faith in himself."

Damon Runyan, well known writer, reportedly said at the time that Marv Owen was a hero in the 1935 World Series in that Owen's hit tied the score in the final game; a fact that was sadly overlooked.

WESTERN UNION

```
Oct. 1935

MARVIN OWEN=
HOTEL WOOLVERINE DET=


CONGRATULATIONS YOUR HIT MEANT THE SERIES AM SO PROUD OF
THE TIGERS=


MOTHER.
```

Here is the telegram from Marv's mother:

World Series 1935 program
(Thanks to Robert D. Opie)

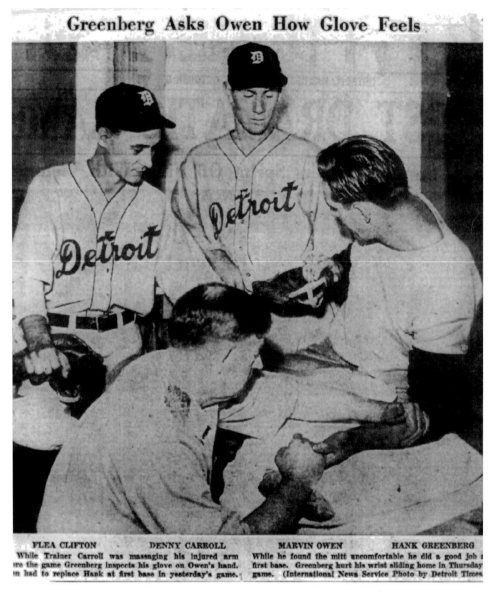

Greenberg Asks Owen How Glove Feels

FLEA CLIFTON DENNY CARROLL MARVIN OWEN HANK GREENBERG
While Trainer Carroll was massaging his injured arm While he found the mitt uncomfortable he did a good job
re the game Greenberg inspects his glove on Owen's hand. first base. Greenberg hurt his wrist sliding home in Thursday
m had to replace Hank at first base in yesterday's game. game. (International News Service Photo by Detroit Times

Hank Injured
(Credit: The Detroit News)

On October 3, during the 1935 World Series, Detroit first sacker Hank Greenberg was injured and Marv on the October 4 game had to move from third to first at the direction of Owner Frank J. Navin. Marv at third had his comfortable finger glove. He tried on Hank's big first base glove. He asked Manager Mickey Cochrane if he could wear his own glove. Mickey was horrified and let Marv know that would be "bush." The next day there were bundles of gloves offered. Mule Haas and Jimmy Dykes of the Chicago White Sox were among those who offered their gloves. Marv finally decided to use Hank's glove. Marv handled first base well and kept the Tiger defense together. He had four assists at 1st base in that single World Series game which at that time was a record. Detroit won the game 6 to 5.

A major leaguer really guards his glove.
In fact with it he falls in love.
With it, he knows any ball it will hold.
It will stay in front of any ball and is bold.
A player knows with that glove on his hand,
He can catch all balls wherever they land.
Player and glove are a team
Together on the same beam.
If glove isn't doing its job and begins to slip,
It is then as useless as a sunken ship.
When glove wears out, player loses a friend.
The player and glove know it's the end.
Before the old glove goes, begin to break in a new one.
When the old glove is gone, with a broken in glove have fun.
The new glove is catching the ball just like before
And the new glove says to each hitter, "Hit me more."

— M. O.

Winning the American League championship in 1935, Detroit went wild with excitement. The Detroit Tigers were heroes and nothing was too good for them. They received honors and invitations by the score. After many social functions, one invitation was to attend a dinner honoring them. Some of the players had other commitments or responsibilities, so only a handful went to the dinner. Marv was one of them. Each of the players at the dinner received the keys to a brand new car (a Chevrolet), Goose Goslin received a pickup truck and the loud applause of the appreciative hosts. You just never know...

This article summarized Owen's skill. Charles P. Ward, Detroit Free Press, columnist wrote *"At third base the Tigers will have Marvin Owen. Last year Owen was the best third sacker in the league, both offensively and defensively. Detroit has come to take Owen for granted. He does his work unobtrusively, so unobtrusively, in fact, that his good points often escape notice. But he is appreciated by rivals who know him as a tricky operator around that bag. And he has a habit of hitting in the pinches. Last year (1936) he drove in 105 runs, and was the only third baseman in the League to send that many tallies across the plate."*

Ripley's — **Believe It or Not!**

"TIGERS' LINEUP"

WHITE
BRIDGES
ROGELL
OWEN
ROWE
GOSLIN

CLIFTON
FOX
NAVIN
CROWDER

COCHRANE
AUKER
GREENBERG

MORGAN
GEHRINGER
WALKER
HAYWORTH

LOYAL TIGER FANS

When asked about his baseball loyalties, Marv replied "I am American League all the way and Detroit is my town. I will always be a Detroit Tiger."

Over the years from the '30's through the '80's and up to 1991, Marv appreciated and responded freely to the fans. Here are some of the reasons why.

Marvin Owen cuts capers on third;
He is great in all sense of the word;
At fielding he rates
As one of the greats,
And all plaudits are justly deserved.

Harry L. Chapper
904 Barrington Road
Grosse Point, Michigan

October 9, 1934

Dear Marvin Owen:

    Please let us present you with a photo of our Little Marvin Owen, whom we are proud to have named after you, hoping that some day he may reach base-ball (sic) fame as you have done.
    We are very sorry that the Tigers lost the World Series this year, and wish you the greatest of luck for next year. We have not lost our faith in you.
    We are very proud of the Tigers, for you have shown wonderful playing ability.
    We have been very proud to have named our son "Marvin Owen" especially now after we have followed you through every game and have seen the wonderful help you have given the Tigers.
    You have become an "Idol" on our street among the little Tiger Fans. They are so fond our own Little Marvin Owen, that they go about shouting, "Marvin Owen is the greatest third baseman that ever played base-ball (sic)."
    Marvin Owen has the chicken pox right now and looks odd with a speckled face, but he'll soon be well again.
    Best wishes to your Mother for we know she is as proud of her son as we are of ours.
Kindly let us know if you receive this photo alright.

                    Two Truly Tiger Fans
                    Mr. & Mrs..............

                Sept. 6, 1934
                Pontiac, Mich.

Mr. Marvin J. Owen.
        Detroit Ball Club, Navin Field
        Detroit, Michigan.

Dear Mr. Owen; Are sending our note to W.JBK in your favor as the most valuable player in the Detroit team.
    So strong is our belief in you being the most valuable player, we have named our sixth son Marvin Owen, in hopes he will be as valuable a man in what ever vocation he chooses in life, as you are to the "Tigers".
    Our boys are great ball fans and are planning strongly to be ball players when grown up and the two older ones are good at bat now. In their games they are home run hitters most of the time.
    Hoping you win in the contest we are
                    Yours truly,
                    Mr & Mrs.............

(Our new son arrived Aug. 31st.)

October 7-1935

Mr. Marvin Owen
Detroit Michigan

Dear Marvin Owen:
        Just to tell you how sorry I felt for you
not getting a hit, so much so that I knelt down
to pray for the dear God to give you one. I
just said;"Please dear God give Owen a hit",
and I heard the smack over the radio and you
scored the tying run..I'm so happy you did not
go hitless, but even tied the score..I thank God
and God bless you.
        It was a great, wonderful series and are
we proud of each and every player? Need I
tell you?..See, what a big part you
played..Tying the score.
                        With sincere good wishes I
                        am
                        excitedly Yours Truly
                        Mrs........................

        May I ask you send your own signature
(autograph) to me? I would forever treasure
it..I think I'll just pray for it. I"m so excited I
can't see straight.

To Marvin Owen

There is a third baseman named Owen,
When he hits the ball he's a goin,
He rounds third base
At a terrible pace
And the people throw hats like its snowin!

by Edgar Hoard, 12 years., Berkley, Michigan

(Ed La Pere, artist, Taylor, MI
Photo: Ross Hamilton, WA)

Gosh, *"Steak"* - that's quite some feat,
Knocking that pill over Cherry Street.
Try eating raw red cabbage,
'Twill surely boost your batting average
Steve
Ypsilanti, Michigan

The headline read, "Owen's Homer in Tenth Beats Yankees."

The Ball Game

'Twas the first inning of the ball game,
And the Yankees were up to bat,
The Yankees went down, one, two, three,
They went down just like that.

For the Yanks Red Ruffing was pitching,
He pitched a terrific game,
Whether the Tigers were up or down
To him it was just the same.

On the mound was Rowe for the Tigers,
He was pitching pretty good ball,
The reason the Yanks made three runs
Was no fault of his at all.

The audience thought the game would last
For many, many suns,
'Til at last the Yankees scored
A scant but needed three runs.

The score was tied at three runs each,
As they went into the tenth inning;
None in the audience even knew
Which team would be winning.

Up came young Marvin Owen to bat,
Determined to connect with the little white ball,
He grabbed a bat, took one peach of a swing,
And drove it over the left field wall.

Written by a loyal Tiger supporter,
Skippy Morris, nine years old,
3911 Buell Ave., Toledo, Ohio

Dedicated to the Tigers and Marvin Owen who won the ball game May 20, 1936.

Detroit Mich
May 26-1936

Mr. Owen

As we are one of the many Radio Baseball fans we are sure pulling for you and the Tigers to repeat for another pennant (sic) for 1936. On Apr. 14th we was blessed with a 10 lb. baby son so me and my wife have decided to name him after you   Marvin Owen ....

Here's for good Luck
Mr. & Mrs........................

Milford, Michigan
Dec. 8, 1937

Mr. Marvin J. Owen.
Dear Marv,

I don't know whether you ball-players like to get fan mail or not so I've never bothered you with any of mine. When I found out management had traded you to Chicago I weakened and thought it wouldn't do any harm to write to you just once and tell you what one fan thinks of you.

I've been going out to Navin Field for the past three years and have always admired you and the way you took care of third base. It sure won't seem the same at the old ball game without you there. I only hope I'll have the good fortune of being at the games when Chicago is here. Believe me I'll still be rooting for you along with the many others who have grown to admire you as I have.

Good luck to you Marv. and heres hoping you have all the success in the world in your new ball club and that in a very short time you'll make W.O. Briggs & Co., regret the day they let the best third baseman in the business leave Michigan and Trumbull Avenues. I remain one of your Most Ardent fans.

Miss.................

Ripley's—**Believe It or Not!**

GERALD WALKER
Detroit Tigers
IN THE
FIRST GAME
OF THE SEASON
HIT A
HOMER
TRIPLE
DOUBLE
SINGLE
IN SUCCESSION
1937

After serving Detroit for five years with distinction, Marv and colorful outfielder Gerry Walker were traded to the Chicago White Sox. What did the Detroit sports writers think about the trade? Let these headlines in the Detroit newspapers speak for themselves.

MORE TIGERS ON BLOCK; FANS ROAR OVER TRADE

ANY GAIN HARD TO FIGURE

TIGER FANS IN UPROAR ON DEALS

TIGERS NEVER WON ON DEAL

MICKEY (COCHRANE) ADMITS WALKER TRADE PUTS HIM ON SPOT

ONLY A FEW FAVOR TRADE

TIGERS MUST WIN PENNANT NEXT SEASON TO JUSTIFY COCHRANE'S DEAL

The White Sox traded players Vernon Kennedy, Tony Piet and Dixie Walker for Marv Owen, Mike Tresh and Gerald Walker of the Tigers.

Among the Western Union telegrams Marv received were these.

> Detroit
> Dec. 1937
> "We're still boiling. However, our loss is Chicago's gain and it will furnish us an excuse to come to Chicago some weekends. Here's hoping you have a grand year with the White Sox. We will be pulling for you."

> Detroit
> Dec. 1937
> "Of all the lousy deals this one takes the prize. All I hope is that the Sox take about four straight flags. Anyway you should be glad to get away from screwballs who would make a trade like that one."

The following correspondence from J. Louis Comiskey and the 1938 Chicago White Sox contract were among the items Marv saved.

CHICAGO WHITE SOX

J. LOUIS COMISKEY, PRESIDENT-TREASURER
HARRY M. GRABINER, VICE PRESIDENT-SECRETARY
JAMES J. DYKES, MANAGER
JOSEPH T. BARRY, TRAVELING SECRETARY

COMISKEY PARK
35TH AND SHIELDS AVENUE
CHICAGO

December 3rd 1937

Mr. Marvin Owens (sic)
362 S. 6th St.
San Jose California

Dear young man:

I am delighted indeed to welcome you to the White Sox and hope you will enjoy playing with our club.

In order to get matters straightened out at once I am enclosing contract herewith calling for $9500 for the 1938 season and ask that you sign same and return it to this office so that we can complete our plans for the coming season.

Kindest regards I am

Very truly yours
J. Louis Comiskey

CHICAGO WHITE SOX

J. LOUIS COMISKEY, PRESIDENT-TREASURER
HARRY M. GRABINER, VICE PRESIDENT-SECRETARY
JAMES J. DYKES, MANAGER
JOSEPH T. BARRY, TRAVELING SECRETARY

COMISKEY PARK
35TH AND SHIELDS AVENUE
CHICAGO

January 22nd 1938

Mr. Marvin Owen
Hotel Como
Hot Springs, Ark.

Dear young man:

Received your signed contract from Mr. Grabiner in California, and am enclosing herewith copy for your files.

I sincerely hope you have a very successful year with us and I assure you we are pleased to have you with us.

Regarding your trip to Hot Springs, as per your arrangements with Mr. Grabiner, we will take care of the expenses of your trip at Hot Springs, and you will be reimbursed when you arrive in Pasadena March 9th.

Wishing you a very pleasant winter and kindest regards I am

Very truly yours
J. Louis Comiskey

IMPORTANT NOTICE

The attention of both Club and Player is specifically directed to the following excerpt from Major League Rule 3(a):

"No Club shall make a contract different from the uniform contract or a contract containing a non-reserve clause, except with the written approval of the Advisory Council. All contracts shall be in duplicate and the Player shall retain a counterpart original. The making of any agreement between a Club and Player not embodied in the contract shall subject both parties to discipline by the Commissioner; and no such agreement, whether written or verbal, shall be recognized or enforced by the Commissioner."

American League of Professional Baseball Clubs

UNIFORM PLAYER'S CONTRACT

Parties   The AMERICAN LEAGUE BASEBALL CLUB OF CHICAGO ILLINOIS
herein called the Club, and   MARVIN J. OWEN   363 S. 6th St.
of San Jose California ...., herein called the Player.

Recital   The Club is a member of the American League of Professional Baseball Clubs. As such, and jointly with the other members of the League, it is a party to the American League Constitution and to agreements and rules with the National League of Professional Baseball Clubs and its constituent clubs, and with the National Association of Professional Baseball Leagues. The purpose of these agreements and rules is to insure to the public wholesome and high-class professional baseball by defining the relations between Club and Player, between club and club, between league and league, and by vesting in a designated Commissioner broad powers of control and discipline, and of decision in case of disputes.

Agreement   In view of the facts above recited the parties agree as follows:

Employment   1. The Club hereby employs the Player to render skilled service as a baseball player in connection with all games of the Club during the year... 1938 including the Club's training season, the Club's exhibition games, the Club's playing season, and the World Series (or any other official series in which the Club may participate and in any receipts of which the player may be entitled to share); and the player covenants that he will perform with diligence and fidelity the service stated and such duties as may be required of him in such employment.

Salary   2. For the service aforesaid the Club will pay the Player an aggregate salary of $ 10,000.00 for seasn (TEN THOUSAND DOLLARS FOR SEASON) as follows:

In semi-monthly installments after the commencement of the playing season covered by this contract, unless the Player is "abroad" with the Club for the purpose of playing games, in which event the amount then due shall be paid on the first week-day after the return "home" of the Club, the terms "home" and "abroad" meaning, respectively, at and away from the city in which the Club has its baseball field.
If a monthly salary is stipulated above, it shall begin with the commencement of the Club's playing season (or such subsequent date as the Player's services may commence) and end with the termination of the Club's scheduled playing season, and shall be payable in semi-monthly installments as above provided.
If the Player is in the service of the Club for part of the playing season only, he shall receive such proportion of the salary above mentioned, as the number of days of his actual employment in the Club's playing season bears to the number of days in said season.

Loyalty   3. (a) The Player will faithfully serve the Club or any other Club to which, in conformity with the agreements above recited, this contract may be assigned, and pledges himself to the American public to conform to high standards of personal conduct, of fair play and good sportsmanship.
(b) The Player represents that he does not, directly or indirectly, own stock or have any financial interest in the ownership or earnings of any Major League club, except as hereinafter expressly set forth, and covenants that he will not hereafter, while connected with any Major League club, acquire or hold any such stock or interest except in accordance with Major League Rule 20 (e).

Service   4. (a) The Player agrees that, while under contract or reservation, he will not play baseball (except post-season games as hereinafter stated) otherwise than for the Club or a Club assignee hereof; that he will not engage in professional boxing or wrestling; and that, except with the written consent of the Club or its assignee, he will not engage in any game or exhibition of football, basketball, hockey or other athletic sport.

Post-season Games   (b) The Player agrees that, while under contract or reservation, he will not play in any post-season baseball games except in conformity with the Major League Rules; and that he will not play in any such baseball game more than ten days after the close of the Major League championship season any year covered by this contract, until the following training season, or in which more than two other players of the Club participate, or with or against any ineligible player or team.

Assignment   5. (a) In case of assignment of this contract to another Club, the Player shall promptly report to the assignee club within 72 hours from the date he receives written notice from the Club of such assignment, if not more than 1600 miles by most-direct available railroad route, plus an additional 24 hours for each additional 800 miles; accrued salary shall be payable when he so reports; and each successive assignee shall become liable to the Player for his salary during his term of service with such assignee, and the Club shall not

83

Chicago White Sox Contract 1938

When he began with Chicago one thing gave him a laugh. In his words, "After I was traded to the White Sox, the Tigers never changed their signs and were using the same signs as when I was with them the year before. Also Gehringer kept his old hit and run sign. Thanks, fellas!"

What would it be like to play for an owner like J. Louis Comiskey and a manager like Jimmy Dykes? It wasn't like Detroit.

Highlights for Marv during the two Chicago years were first, his friendships with pitchers Monty Stratton and Thornton Lee and second, his participation representing the Chicago White Sox, in the Baseball Centennial Celebration at Cooperstown, June 12, 1939.

Monty Stratton whose baseball career was tragically ended in a hunting accident was admired by Marv and the two enjoyed a friendship. Thornton Lee, another Chicago pitcher, became a lifelong friend. The Owen family and the Lee family kept in touch through correspondence for over fifty years.

This invitation was sent in
June 1939 to four Chicago
White Sox players
including Marv. An
invitation was also sent to
Hank Greenberg with the
Detroit Tigers.

**AMERICAN LEAGUE
PROFESSIONAL BASEBALL CLUBS**
310 SOUTH MICHIGAN BUILDING
CHICAGO

June 7, 1939

To: Mr. Lyons, Owen, Ruel, Stratton:

In the program for the Baseball Centennial Celebration, to be held at Cooperstown, New York, on Monday, June 12th, there will be a cavalcade of baseball, winding up with a Major League game played between selected players from the National and American Leagues. You have been selected from Chicago as one of the members of the team.

All of our scheduled games have been cancelled for this day.

You will be furnished with railroad and Pullman transportation from Chicago to Cooperstown and Cooperstown to Washington, where you are scheduled to again join the Chicago Club on Wednesday, June 14th.

You will leave on the New York Central (Lake Shore Limited) at 5:30 P.M. railroad time, 6:30 Chicago daylight saving time, Sunday. If you prefer, you could board this train at Englewood where it is scheduled to leave at 6:43. This train is scheduled to arrive in Utica at 9:45 A.M., Monday morning, where a special stop will be made. Automobile service will be furnished you from Utica to Cooperstown.

At Cooperstown we will make our headquarters at the Cooper Inn during the day.

On the return trip, the entire party will leave Cooperstown at six o'clock, making connection at Albany for New York and Boston, as well as points West. It will probably be necessary for you to remain in New York overnight as you will not arrive there until midnight, and rejoin your club in Washington on Tuesday. Tuesday is an open date in the American League schedule.

You will be reimbursed for your incidental expenses including hotel at New York, meals, taxi cab hire, etc.

Kindly bring with you your gray road uniform, your baseball shoes, bats, gloves and whatever other paraphernalia you will need for the playing of the game.

Please see that your uniform is in perfect condition so that the American League players will make a splendid appearance on the field.

Please ignore any communication you may have received from Steve Hannagan or Al Stoughton of the National Baseball Centennial Commission in regard to train service, etc. to Cooperstown, and follow the above instructions.

Will appreciate acknowledgment of this assignment.

Sincerely yours,

William Harridge
President.

June 12, 1939 marked the Cavalcade of Baseball at Cooperstown, N.Y. where the National Baseball Museum and the Hall of Fame were formally dedicated at the birthplace of the game.

Eleven members of the Hall of Fame attended: Nap Lajoie, George Sisler, Cy Young, Tris Speaker, Walter Johnson, Honus Wagner, Connie Mack, Grover Cleveland Alexander, Eddie Collins, Ty Cobb and Babe Ruth. Lou Gehrig was ill.

In attendance and participating were: K.M. Landis, Commissioner of Baseball, Ford Frick, President of the National League, William Harridge, President of the American League.

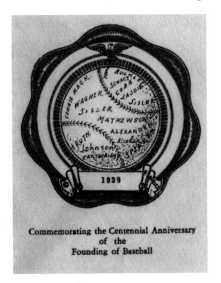

Commemorating the Centennial Anniversary
of the
Founding of Baseball

The seven inning baseball game played in celebration of the event was composed of star players captained by two Hall of Famers: Eddie Collins and Honus Wagner. Here are the lineups:

Wagner's Team
Wally Moses - Athletics
Lloyd Waner - Pirates
Arky Vaughn - Pirates
Charley Gehringer - Tigers
Joe Medwick - Cards
Mel Ott - Giants
Moe Berg - Red Sox
Jimmy Wilson - Reds
Marv Owen - White Sox
Lefty Grove - Red Sox
Danny Macfayden - Bees
Johnny Allen - Indians

Collin's Team
Billy Herman - Cubs
Stan Hack - Cubs
Hank Greenberg - Tigers
George Selkirk - Yankees
Art Jorgens - Yankees
Cecil Travis - Senators
Dizzy Dean - Cubs
Johnny Vander Meer - Reds
Syl Johnson - Phillies
Frankie Hayes - Athletics
Muddy Ruel - White Sox

Wagner's Team won 4-2.

1939 Hall of Fame Dedication

The picture shows 10 inductees at the 1939 Hall of Fame Dedication: Front Row— Eddie Collins, Babe Ruth, Connie Mack, Cy Young
Back Row— Honus Wagner, Grover Cleveland, Tris Speaker, Nap Lajoie, George Sisler, Walter Johnson
Note: Lou Gehrig was seriously ill and could not attend.
(National Library and Archive, Cooperstown, N.Y.)

95

Marv, then with the Chicago White Sox, looked forward to the Baseball Centennial Celebration at Cooperstown, New York. Also invited was Hank Greenberg from the Detroit Tigers. Marv and Hank were greatly impressed by the eleven Hall of Fame charter members who were lined up at home plate: Walter Johnson, Babe Ruth, Ty Cobb, Tris Speaker, George Sisler, Ed. T. Collins, Nap "Larry" Lajoie, Honus Wagner, Cy Young, G.C. "Pete" Alexander and Connie Mack. Lou Gehrig was ill and unable to attend the Celebration.

Hank mentioned to Marv that he had two official baseballs with him and surely would like to have them autographed but said he was too bashful. Marv, who was not known for being especially outgoing, said, "Let me go do it." Marv walked up to each Hall of Famer and each signed the two balls. Later, Marv said that each of the eleven Hall of Famers was very good about signing. Hank kept one autographed ball and gave one to Marv who kept it in a fur-lined glove in a safe deposit box.

Marv's second season with Chicago was cut short when George Case slid into 3rd base and Marv's hand was broken.

In December 1939 at the annual major league meetings, the Chicago White Sox sold Marv to the Boston Red Sox for an undisclosed amount of cash. A highlight of that major league meeting was the failure of legislation to curb the power of Commissioner Kenesaw M. Landis, a man Marv viewed as the advocate for the players.

Three people with Boston who impressed Marv were the Owner Thomas A. Yawkey, Manager Joe Cronin and outfielder, Dom DiMaggio who became his roommate. The two were ideal roommates—quiet and shy.

Baseball Commissioner Kenesaw Mountain Landis
(Thanks to: Rev. Jerome C. Romanowski, Holy Name Society)

Initially at Boston, Marv was used as a utility infielder and then after a bad foot injury began his career as a Boston Red Sox coach. From his early days at Santa Clara College he had studied to be a teacher and a coach, so it was about ten years after his college graduation that he put his training to work.

His chosen lifelong occupation from childhood to adulthood was always related to baseball. First as a player then progressively as a coach, player-manager, manager, scout and then in retirement a volunteer teacher/mentor to young Santa Clara University baseball players.

Marv summed up his time in Chicago and Boston: "Spent a couple of seasons in Windy City, Illinois. When shipped out of there said, 'Oh Boy!' Then spent one season in Massachusetts. Outside of good seafood there, the state gave me fits!"

In 1940 Marv obtained his release from Boston as a free agent, thanks to the efforts of Commissioner Kenesaw Mountain Landis. According to Marv, "I called Judge Landis at his hotel and told him I was benched. He said, 'Come see me at my hotel.' After I had told him the circumstances, he said I had a case. He then got in touch with the management and said give this man a job or give him free agency. I received a wire from management asking if I would accept free agency. I sent back a one word response, 'Yes.' I signed with Portland, three years as a player, and three years as a player/manager, winning the Coast League title in 1945. The Judge was the ball player's best friend! He didn't give a snap of his fingers who the involved parties were. He'd go to bat for a minor league player as quickly as for an outstanding big-timer."

Violet and Marv read about Boston.

When Marv graduated from college, baseball was his only goal. However, throughout his career, as he matured, he became a teacher/mentor to younger players. This was evidenced when he was a player/manager, manager, scout or as a volunteer coach at the Santa Clara University. He was always teaching.

From 1941 to 1946 Marv was with Portland of the Pacific Coast League, doubling as player-manager his last three seasons. He was highly successful in his managerial debut, finishing second in 1944 and winning the pennant in 1945.

When Marv managed Portland, anytime the team won 7 games in a row, everyone was invited to a complete steak dinner at the manager's house. His wife was an excellent cook!

In 1945 he held the highest fielding average in the history of the Pacific Coast League at that time .986 and a batting average of .311. He was manager/third baseman of the Portland Beavers and led the Beavers to the Pacific Coast League pennant that year.

He piloted San Jose in the Red Sox system for five years and then, in 1952, came back to the Tigers, managing their Davenport, Durham and Valdosta clubs until July 1, 1954, when he was moved into the Detroit scouting department.

In managing and scouting, Marv always emphasized in his coaching the importance of the players' hands.

Portland Beavers third baseman and manager

In teaching rookie infielders, these were the pointers stressed:

1. The slow roller: you start quickly, run fast, keep control of your legs. Your legs and hands must work together. They can't fight each other. The ball has to be caught 3 ways: left side one hand, backhand and bare hand. The infielder must have agility and ability plus good hands. By that I mean quick hands, flexible and easy hands, sure and strong hands.

2. The other grounder is the short hop, baby hop or in pro ball the TRAP. This is the most difficult grounder to catch if you do not break correctly. If you break correctly, it is the easiest ball to catch. When you make the trap, this is what happens:
   - you play the ball instead of the ball playing you,
   - the trap eliminates the bad hop; you kill it before it grows,
   - the trap puts you in throwing position,
   - you get the ball sooner, and it gives you more time to throw,
   - the trap also makes it a shorter throw.

Other reminders:
   - Use your glove if the sun is in your eyes;
   - Break for the ball in the hole;
   - 2nd baseman and shortstop should have the ball caught 50 feet before it gets to them.
   - The third baseman should bare hand the 2nd throw from the 1st baseman when the pitcher is warming up; 2nd baseman and shortstop should do the same, then it becomes routine.
   - When ball zigs, you zig, and when the ball zags, you zag. If the ball zigs and you zag, that

is another error for you.
   - An infielder will make his usual amount of errors annually, so don't make a careless one by being nonchalant on a ball.
   - Don't catch with concrete hard hands; catch with soft, easy hands.

These were some of the stories Marv told about his days in Portland.

My base runner was called out at first base. I complained. The umpire said, "From where did you see the play?" I replied, "From the third base dugout." The ump came back with "Do you mean you can see a play from there better than I can from here?" I said, "I could see it better than you can if I were behind the right field fence."

At Portland, a large sewer line was put through centerfield while the club was on the road. The day before we arrived home in Portland, a heavy rain fell, but the game was played the next day. About the 3rd inning, we noticed there was no visiting centerfielder — all we could see was a glove, sticking out of a big hole in centerfield. The rain made the earth sink.

One of my favorite plays happened when I was playing third base for the Portland Beavers in the Pacific Coast League. Our team had an outfielder with a less than strong arm. This time there was a man on first and the batter hit to the outfielder. As the runner went to second and then started to third, I was ready for the ball which was slow in coming. I got the ball at the edge of the webbing of my glove and slapped the ball on the runner who was sliding into third. I dropped the ball and the ball and my hand were under the runner. I had no idea where the ball was. The umpire yelled, 'OUT.' I let out a scream of pain, dropped my glove and ran about holding my wrist. Meanwhile, I let the shortstop

"There are two grounders you have to handle 99 times out of 100. To be a better infielder, you have to practice making these plays day after day.

know I was okay. Our manager, Oscar Vitt caught on, so he yelled out, "Take your time, Marv. If you can stay in, we need you." After a little time I returned to my place at third; the runner was still out despite his protests."

As a player/manager I was generally low key, not a fighting, quick-tempered type. This changed during a game in Portland. In fact, the press dispatch labeled the incident a "Bulletin" when it came in over the wires from Los Angeles. It was big news June 9, 1944, because after a beef with the umpire I was thrown out of a game... One newspaper columnist even described me as a hardboiled skipper.

At an Oakland-Portland Beavers Pacific Coast League game at Oakland, July 26 in the 1940's, a strange thing happened. With one out in the frame, Portland filled the sacks. Mayo Smith then hit a grand slam; Walt Flager then hit a double. The players in the dugout looked at the right scoreboard which showed two outs when actually there was only one. The next batter Glen Crawford flied out. The Beavers hustled out to the field. No one noticed the mistake in outs. The umpires didn't notice it either!

When Marv was asked about the chances of the Beavers he said, "We'll get going;" Then he said, "the beavers, sure we'll get going'—

How can we help it with a Cohen (lefthanded pitcher) and an Owen?"

I was only "booted" out of one game after 13 seasons; I wouldn't complain unless there was a legitimate reason and the umpires knew that.

This is the telegram.

WESTERN UNION

June 12, 1944

SEATTLE WASH

MARVIN OWEN=C/O KLEPPER BALL PARK MANAGER BASE BALL CLUB
PORTLAND ORG= YOU ARE FINED FIFTY DOLLARS FOR YOUR USE OF ABUSIVE LANGUAGE TO
UMPIRE FORD AND ALSO FOR DELAYING THE PLAYING OF BALL GAME ON FRIDAY NIGHT JUNE
9TH. REMIT FIVE IMMEDIATELY=
CLARENCE ROWLAND.

During the World War II years, baseball players were hard to find due to the war manpower needs. On the Portland Beaver teams beginning in 1941, many players were 4-F or over-age for the military. Marv was 4-F(H) due to health. He stated at the time, "Maybe Klepper (General Manager for Portland) isn't so dumb by going out and signing 4-F's and over-age players. In the long run this method may pay dividends." It did in 1945 when Portland won the Pacific Coast League Pennant.

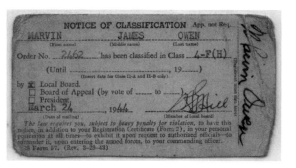

1945-4F (H)

Marv Led Pacific Coast League third basemen in fielding:

1941	FA	.954
1944	FA	.964
1945	FA	.986

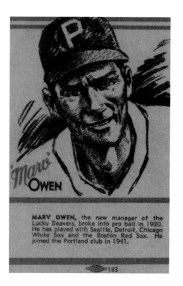

MARV OWEN, the new manager of the Lucky Beavers, broke into pro ball in 1930. He has played with Seattle, Detroit, Chicago White Sox and the Boston Red Sox. He joined the Portland club in 1941.

MARV OWEN Portland Statistics
1941 through 1946

Year	G	AB	R	H	2B	3B	HR	RBI	BA	SA	TB	SB
1941 Player	144	501	68	150	38	6	1	70	.299	.405	203	3
1942	147	535	52	162	27	7	3	66	.303	.396	212	5
1943	73	260	27	80	12	2	0	32	.308	.369	96	1
1944 Player/Mgr.	131	449	40	130	27	2	1	63	.290	.365	164	9
1945	163	566	88	176	40	3	1	83	.311	.398	225	10
1946	39	103	8	16	1	1	0	5	.155	.184	19	0
Totals	835	2857	350	847	169	28	9	374	.296	.385	1099	44

Thanks to Dick Dobbins,
Alamo, CA

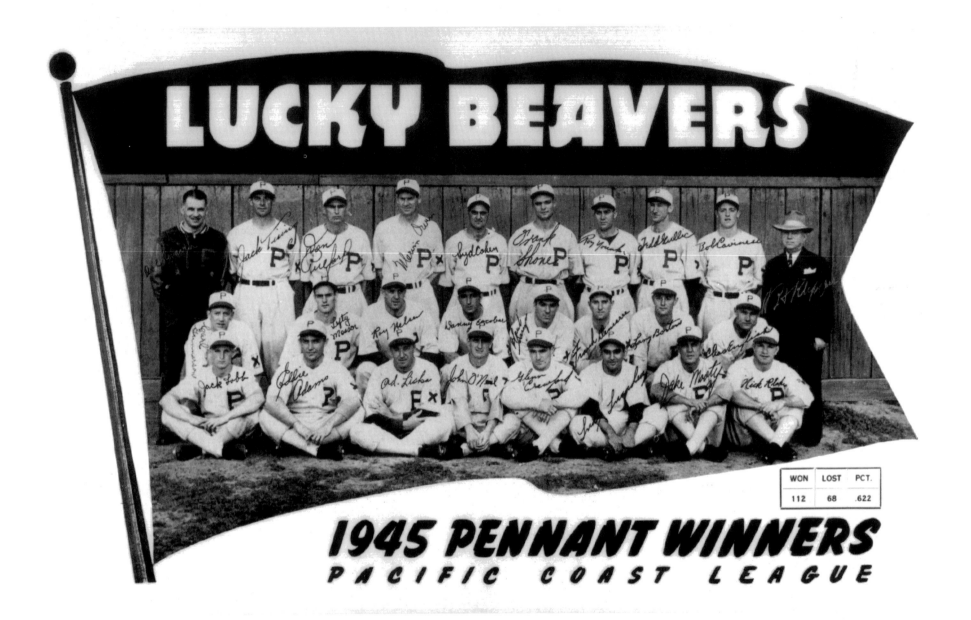

WON	LOST	PCT.
112	68	.622

1945 PENNANT WINNERS
PACIFIC COAST LEAGUE

"Lucky" Beavers
1945 HOME GAMES

Hollywood
APRIL 17, 18, 19, 20, 21, 22-22
JULY 17, 18, 19, 20, 21, 22-22

Oakland
APRIL 24, 25, 26, 27, 28, 29-29
AUG. 14, 15, 16, 17, 18, 19-19

Los Angeles
MAY 15, 16, 17, 18, 19, 20-20
AUG. 21, 22, 23, 24, 25, 26-26

San Francisco
MAY 22, 23, 24, 25, 26, 27-27
JULY 10, 11, 12, 13, 14, 15-15

Seattle
JUNE 12, 13, 14, 15, 16, 17-17
AUG. 7, 8, 9, 10, 11, 12-12

Sacramento
JUNE 19, 20, 21
SEPT. 18, 19, 20, 21, 22, 23-23

San Diego
JUNE 22, 23, 24-24
SEPT. 11, 12, 13, 14, 15, 16-16

MARV OWEN
NIGHT
Seals Stadium
SEPT. 7, 1945

SAN JOSE

EAGLES

SPONSORS

The Fraternal order of Eagles arranged a Marv Owen Night at Seals Stadium for San Jose fans.

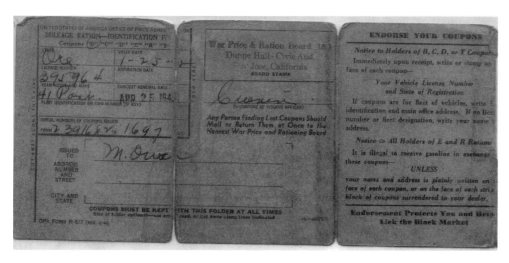

Gasoline rationing coupons

April 1943
Registered, but was rejected

From Portland Beavers 1945 Scorecard

During the war years, Oregon became a major shipbuilding state. Mrs. Marvin Owen (Violet), was invited to sponsor the "S.S. Niantic Victory," a ship built by the Oregon Shipbuilding Corporation for the United States Maritime Commission. The "Niantic Victory" ship and the Portland Beavers Baseball Club were called the future champions from Portland. Violet and Marv are pictured here at the luncheon celebrating the event on April 25, 1944. Marv was player/manager for the Portland Beavers (Pacific Coast League) at the time.

1946 Portland Beavers Program

Marvin John Owen, third baseman and manager. Is managing club for man who started him out in baseball. When "Bland Bill" Klepper owned the Seattle Club, Owen was recommended to him by Scout Justin Fitzgerald, the former Seal outfielder, and one of the fastest men ever seen on the diamond. Marvin was born in San Jose, Calif., Mar. 22, 1908. Nickname, "Marv." Attended high school Santa Clara, Calif., and Santa Clara College. Starred in baseball in both schools. Signed with Seattle as a first baseman, but played his first professional game as a third baseman, and the "hot corner" proved to be his natural position, which carried him to a long career in the majors and fastest minors. Feels that he owes most in baseball to the early influence of his father and mother because of their interest in the game, and their encouragement. Baseball ambition, to win a pennant. Otherwise, to be a success in business. Says his greatest baseball thrill came early. He says, **"That was when I was a rookie in the American league, and Babe Ruth, walking past me on the field, said 'hello' to me."** Toughest thing in baseball for an infielder is to judge and snare a bad "hop"—at least, in his experience.

"Lucky Beaver" Roster for 1946

Player's Name	Position	Place and Date of Birth	Ht.	Wt.	Thrs.	Bats
LISKA, ADOLPH J.	Pitcher	Dwight, Neb.—July 10, 1907	5.11	166	R.	R.
HELSER, ROY H.	Pitcher	Portland, Ore.—Aug. 27, 1915	5.09	195	L.	L.
PULFORD, BERT DONALD	Pitcher	Minneapolis, Minn.—April 1, 1916	6.01	184	R.	R.
BARRETT, RICHARD	Pitcher	Monticreville, Pa.—Sept. 28, 1908	5.09	170	R.	R.
SALVESON, JOHN T., JR.	Pitcher	Fullerton, Calif.—Jan. 15, 1914	6.01	205	R.	R.
MOOTY, JAKE I.	Pitcher	Bennett, Texas—April 13, 1914	5.11	170	R.	R.
COHEN, SYDNEY	Pitcher	Baltimore, Md.—May 7, 1909	5.11	150	L.	S.
ORRELL, GORDON F.	Pitcher	National City, Calif.—Oct. 6, 1918	6.04	210	R.	R.
TISING, JOHN	Pitcher	—1907	6.02	190	R.	L.
HOLM, WILLIAM F.	Catcher	Chicago, Ill.—July 21, 1913	5.11	185	R.	R.
ADAMS, EDWARD F.	Catcher	Rudyard, Mont.—April 13, 1918	5.10	185	R.	R.
BARTON, LAWRENCE	Infielder	Gray, Kansas—Nov. 21, 1913	5.11	185	L.	L.
BUCHER, JAMES Q.	Infielder	Manassa, Va.—Mar. 24, 1912	5.11	160	R.	R.
STRANGE, ALAN C.	Infielder	Philadelphia, Pa.—Nov. 7, 1909	5.09	160	R.	R.
BROWN, JOHN I.	Infielder	Mason, Texas—July 22, 1913	5.11	165	R.	R.
WHEELER, EDWARD R.	Infielder	Los Angeles, Calif.—May 15, 1919	5.09	155	R.	R.
OWEN, MARVIN J.	Infielder	San Jose, Calif., Mar. 22, 1908	6.01	178	R.	R.
FLAGER, WALTER	Infielder	Chicago, Ill.—Nov. 3, 1921	5.11	160	R.	L.
REICH, HERMAN	Outfielder	Bell, Calif.—Nov. 23, 1917	6.02	195	L.	R.
GOUISH, NICK E.	Outfielder	Punsutawney, Pa.—Nov. 13, 1918	6.01	188	L.	L.
ESCOBAR, DANIEL	Outfielder	San Jose, Calif.—Sept. 29, 1916	5.11	178	L.	L.
AMARAL, EDWARD D.	Outfielder	San Jose, Calif.—May 18, 1915	6.00	175	R.	R.
GULLIC, TEDD J.	Outfielder	Koshkonong, Mo.—Jan. 2, 1907	6.02	185	R.	R.
SHONE, FRANK	Outfielder	Pittsburgh, Pa.—1920	6.02	180	R.	R.
SMITH, MAYO	Outfielder	New London, Mo.—Jan. 17, 1915	6.00	182	R.	L.
CARNEY, WILLIAM	Outfielder	Portland, Ore.—Aug. 14, 1920	6.01	185	R.	L.

Marv was the first manager of the San Jose team in the California League after the city was given a franchise in 1947. He guided the San Jose Red Sox into second place in San Jose's first full season in organized baseball. The team was in 6th place on July 4 and ended the season in second place.

Fans enjoyed day games and night games at the Municipal Baseball Park in San Jose. Opening night often drew over 3,000 who came to welcome back veteran players like Ernie Sierra and Ed Sobczak, and to encourage the rookies. The players and the fans were friendly; the games had a small town feeling.

Municipal Baseball Park, San Jose, CA
(Thanks to San Jose Chamber of Commerce)

Manager San Jose Red Sox
1947 through 1951

107

The Smiling San Jose Red Sox
Marv is front row, second on leftside.

Six years earlier, in 1941, Buddy Leitch, Sports Editor for the San Jose News had written this prophetic letter to Freck (Marv). Little did Leitch realize that he was forecasting an event (Marv managing a San Jose Class C franchise). As it turned out the San Jose team's parent club was the Boston Red Sox and not Portland.

Here is that 1941 letter:

SAN JOSE NEWS

AN INDEPENDENT NEWSPAPER
BY
G. LOGAN PAYNE

66-76 W. San Antonio St.
SAN JOSE, CALIF.

April 1, 1941.

Dear Freck:

This is not an April 1st joke, rather it's serious business.

There's a story kicking around here that has the Portland Club in line for the San Jose Class C franchise next year and should this develop YOU will be placed in charge of said team. It is also reported that you signed with Portland with this thought in mind.

In some ways, this sounds pretty weak, but on the other hand who knows what may develop in pro baseball. This is your home town and you may want to settle down locally. In this business we have to check on such reports. You know how it is.

In your spare time, drop me a line and put me on the right track, will you please?

Guess you are itching to get into action so that the first and 15th days of the month will mean something. Oscar Vitt gave you a nice boost over the UP wire today--and indication you enjoyed a good session in camp.

Nothing exciting here, Marv. Lots of rain, so not much doing in sports.

Lots of luck and gobs of success. Keep me posted.

Buddy Leitch
sports editor

In 1948 at the annual Banquet of Champions, Marv was awarded the highest honor — 1947 Champion of Champions in recognition of his management of the 1947 San Jose Red Sox. Accepting the award before approximately 400 award attendees, Owen said, "It's a thrill of thrills for me. I feel like the fellow who said I'm dreaming with my eyes wide open. I really don't think I deserve this outstanding award that has been given to me tonight." The audience gave him a great ovation and approval.

Afterwards Marv said he was more nervous going to the speaker's table to accept the trophy than when he played in the 1934 World Series.

CALIFORNIA LEAGUE'S TOP TWENTY ALL-TIME WINNING MANAGERS
(through the 1995 season)

Manager (Total Years Managed)	Wins
1. Donald "Ducky" LeJohn (7years)	482
2. Ray Petty (6 years)	466
3. John "Red" Marion (5 years)	385
4. Marv Owen (5 years)	377*
Greg Mahlberg (6 years)	377
6. Roland LeBlanc (5 years)	366
Harry Dunlop (5 years)	366
8. Duane Espy (4 years)	321
9. Ted Kubiak (5 years)	309
10. John Van Orum (4 years)	301
11. Gene Lillard (4 years)	295
12. William Werle (4 years)	284
13. Harry Malmberg (4 years)	274
14. Scott Ullger (3 years)	254
15. Tom Kotcham (3 years)	248
16. Wendell Kim (3 years)	240
17. Roy Partee (3 years)	238
18. R.J. Harrison (3 years)	235
19. George Mitterwald (3 years)	234
20. Tom Beyers (3 years)	233
Stan Wasiak (3 years)	233

*Only 3 managers in California League history won more games than Marv Owen.

Contributed by Rick Smith
Bakersfield, CA

California League Standings 1947 through 1951

1947 CLUB	W	L	PCT.	MANAGER
Stockton	95	45	.679	John Babich
Visalia	79	61	.564	John Intlekofer
San Jose	79	61	.564	Marvin Owen
Santa Barbara	73	67	.521	Ray Hathaway
Bakersfield	66	74	.471	Antone Governor
Ventura	58	82	.414	Michael Gazella, John Sturm
Fresno	58	82	.414	Frank Demaree, Wm. Harris, Chas. Baron, Wm. Brenzel
Modesto	52	88	.371	Harry Green

PLAYOFF - Stockton defeated San Jose, 3 games to 0; Santa Barbara defeated Visalia, 3 games to 0; Stockton defeated Santa Barbara, 4 games to 0.

1948 CLUB	W	L	PCT.	MANAGER
Fresno	85	55	.607	A. Stanley Benjamin
Ventura	80	60	.571	Edward Kearse
Santa Barbara	74	66	.529	Chester Kehn
Stockton	72	68	.514	Vincent DiMaggio
Modesto	70	70	.500	William Jackson
Bakersfield	70	70	.500	Harry Griswold
San Jose	64	76	.457	Marvin Owen
Visalia	45	95	.321	John Intlekofer, Arnold Statz, Donald Anderson

PLAYOFF - Santa Barbara defeated Fresno, 3 games to 2; Stockton defeated Ventura, 3 games to 0; Santa Barbara defeated Stockton, 4 games to 3.

1949 CLUB	W	L	PCT.	MANAGER
Bakersfield	85	54	.612	Harry Griswold
Fresno	83	57	.593	Bernard (Frenchy) Uhalt
Ventura	80	60	.571	Battle (Bones) Sanders
San Jose	76	64	.543	Marvin Owen
Santa Barbara	75	65	.536	Chester Kehn
Stockton	64	76	.457	Anthony (Nino) Bongiovanni
Modesto	54	85	.388	William Jackson, Max Macon
Visalia	42	98	.300	T. Leon Treadway, Arnold Statz, Claude Passeau

PLAYOFF - Ventura defeated Bakersfield, 3 games to 2; San Jose defeated Fresno, 3 games to 0; San Jose defeated Ventura, 4 games to 1.

1950 CLUB	W	L	PCT.	MANAGER
Ventura	85	55	.607	R. Eugene Lillard
Modesto	82	58	.586	Marcus Carrola
Stockton	79	61	.564	Harry Clements
San Jose	78	62	.557	Marvin Owen
Visalia	65	75	.464	James Acton
Bakersfield	61	79	.436	Harry Griswold
Fresno	58	82	.414	Roland LeBlanc
Santa Barbara	52	88	.371	William Hart

PLAYOFF - Modesto defeated San Jose, 3 games to 1; Stockton defeated Ventura, 3 games to 2; Modesto defeated Stockton, 4 games to 1.

1951 CLUB	W	L	PCT.	MANAGER
Santa Barbara	88	59	.599	William Hart
San Jose	80	67	.544	Marvin Owen
Stockton	79	68	.537	Harry Clements
Visalia	76	71	.517	James Trew, V. Cecil Garriott
Modesto	74	73	.503	Antonio Freitas
Ventura	72	75	.490	R. Eugene Lillard
Fresno	61	86	.414	Larry Barton
Bakersfield	58	89	.395	Wellington (Wimpy) Quinn

PLAYOFF - Santa Barbara defeated Stockton, 3 games to 1; Visalia defeated San Jose, 3 games to 1; Santa Barbara defeated Visalia, 4 games to 1.

The Trap Wall

In 1958 when Marv was a Detroit Tiger scout at Tigertown, Florida, he designed and supervised construction of the Trap Wall, a 9 feet high and 19 feet wide wall and a 16 feet slab extending out from the wall to sharpen fielding skills of infielders. Players threw the ball against the wall (it was something like a handball court), charged the ball and then learned to pick it up with the glove just above the ground, so there were no bad hops, the player was in a better position to throw and had more time to execute the play. Initially the wall was called "Owen's Folly" until it was noticed that fielders were improving their "trap" skills and pitchers were also making use of the wall.

Marv got the idea for the trap wall because as a player he had to learn the hard way. He watched teammate Charlie Gehringer, Detroit star 2nd baseman who was a master of the trap play. Remembering that is what motivated Marv to come up with the innovative Trap Wall.

Jim Campbell, former President of the Tigers, reported that the wall was still in use in 1983, but the wall is no longer there now.

DETROIT TIGERS

TIGER STADIUM • DETROIT, MICHIGAN 48216 • (313) 962-4000

May 18, 1993

Dear Viola:

It was good to chat with you the other day. Marv was a good friend of mine - a real gentleman. Charlie and Jo Gehringer often mentioned the good times they shared with Marv.

David Miller, our Director of Minor League Operations, has been out of town and upon his return I asked about the nine foot wall that Marv was instrumental in having erected at our spring training minor league complex in Lakeland, Florida. Dave told me that The Trap was torn down at least 5-6 years ago as it was not being used.

Kind regards.

Sincerely,

DETROIT TIGERS, INC.

Alice Sloane
Senior Director
Administration

Marv, Detroit Tiger Scout, with Charlie Dressen, Tiger Manager looking at prospects, 1963

In a Dan Hruby column in the San Jose Mercury, Mar. 29, 1971, Marv described some of the perils of scouting. He told about having his tires slashed during a game in Los Angeles, his fan belt cut in Glendale. One of the scariest was after a game in Bakersfield. He left the night game early and on an isolated road, a station wagon roared up behind him with the car's bright lights on him and the horn blowing continuously. The driver signaled for Marv to pull over, but knowing it wasn't the Highway Patrol and seeing four guys on the floor of the station wagon, Marv decided he wasn't hanging around. The driver of the station wagon tried to run him off the road. At this point Marv decided to make a really fast get away, which he did. Luckily after a few miles he came to an arterial stop where there were other cars. The station wagon turned off.

When Marv arrived back at his motel, he told the desk clerk what happened. The clerk told him a few nights previously five hoodlums had stopped, robbed and beaten a lone motorist on the same road Marv had just left.

III. TIGER TALES—LOOKING BACK

Several times a week in the late 1980's, Marv's son, Skip, Skip's wife, Joan and Marv's Sister, Babe, would individually visit him at the retirement community where he lived. Usually, current sport page stories or baseball magazine articles were the topic of conversation. Most of the stories that follow were results of those conversations. Something he read would remind Marv of how it used to be and the following variety of topics were what unfolded.

Marv liked to recall favorite memories from his baseball career. Here, in his words, are some of those that he enjoyed remembering and retelling.

In 1930 in my first year of professional baseball, I was playing shortstop. When I came to bat I hit a hot line drive to left field. The ball landed on my glove in the field. I went to first and one of my teammates scored. In those days, players left their gloves on the field when they went up to bat.

In 1931 during my first spring training, Detroit was playing the San Francisco Seals. This is the play that occurred and if TV cameras had been there then, they would have captured the most outstanding play for action on one pitched ball. There was just one pitched ball. At the time of the pitch there was only one runner on base. There were 5 throws (not counting the one by the pitcher), 5 slides, 1 error, 1 run and a runner left on third base. This is how it went: the hitter had 3 balls and 2 strikes on him. On the pitch, the runner on 1st base was on his way to steal 2nd base; when the pitcher threw the pitch, the umpire was slow in calling it and the catcher thought it was a strike. Before the umpire made his call, the catcher threw the ball to the second baseman trying to get the man stealing second. When the hitter saw that the throw to 2nd base was going to go to centerfield, he dashed to first base. The original runner on 1st base slid into 2nd base but when he saw the ball go to centerfield he went sliding safely into 3rd. The throw was too late. In the meantime the hitter now is running to 2nd base and slides safely into that base. The throw is too late. Meanwhile the runner at third base picked himself up and goes safely into home plate. The throw is too late. The runner on second decides to go to third, the throw is too late, and the runner is safe.

A few, quite a few years ago, the Santa Clara University baseball team won three league games in one day. They started the day off with a tied game from the day before. It went a few innings and in the concluding inning Santa Clara won. Following that, the two universities played a double header and Santa Clara won both; total for the day: three victories!

I have never seen this oddity in professional baseball, but in scouting I saw this three times - once in high school, once in jr. college and once in a four year college: five left handed players in the lineup at one time: 1st base, pitcher, right, center and left fields.

In a regular major league game, I saw 9 right handed hitters face a team of 9 left handed hitters. Not one of the many newspapers for that city mentioned the oddity in their papers. I kept the box score of that game in my baseball memorabilia for many years.

115

In the 1961 All Star Game in Boston, the American League sent four Tigers up to hit successively at one point: Jim Bunning was batting 9th and was followed by Norm Cash, Rocky Colavito and Al Kaline.

This unique feat I first read about in the Portland Oregonian August 28, 1941, and I've saved this article for over 49 years. Here is how it was reported in the Oregonian.

MANITOWOC, Wis., Aug. 27 (AP)—Stone McGlynn, who died this week claimed one of baseball's most unusual feats—retiring the opposition, who had loaded the bases with none out, without once throwing to the batter.

"The St. Louis Cardinals were playing Cincinnati in 1907," McGlynn recounted recently. "The Reds whaled our starting pitcher and got off to a big lead."

"Manager John McCloskey called on Bugs Raymond, the greatest spitballer that ever pitched. Bugs loaded the sacks with nobody out and got three balls and no strikes on the next batter.
Runners Picked Off
"McCloskey said: 'Stoney, you'd better go in there and stop 'em.' I said, "Hell, John, there's no use sending me in now; they got us licked.' He insisted and I finally went in."

Stoney said that the first thing he did was to catch Hans Lobert, now coach for the Philadelphia Nationals, off third base. Then he caught the runner off second and finally nipped the man off first.
"That's the gospel truth," McGlynn said of his favorite story. "I retired the side without pitching to the batter."

(Credit: "Tiger Tales")

"The first Detroit Tigers Old Timers game took place June 28, 1958 against the Boston Red Sox at Briggs Stadium. Charlie Gehringer, Billy Rogell and I were in the infield and in the outfield were Pete Fox, Jo-Jo White and Goose Goslin - all members of the Tiger pennant teams of 1934 and 1935. Nine Hall of Famers in the game were Cobb, Gehringer, Crawford, Mickey Cochrane, Joe Cronin, Lefty Grove and Jimmy Foxx. The game was two innings only and ended in a 1-1 tie."

"Here is the letter of invitation that I've saved since 1958!"

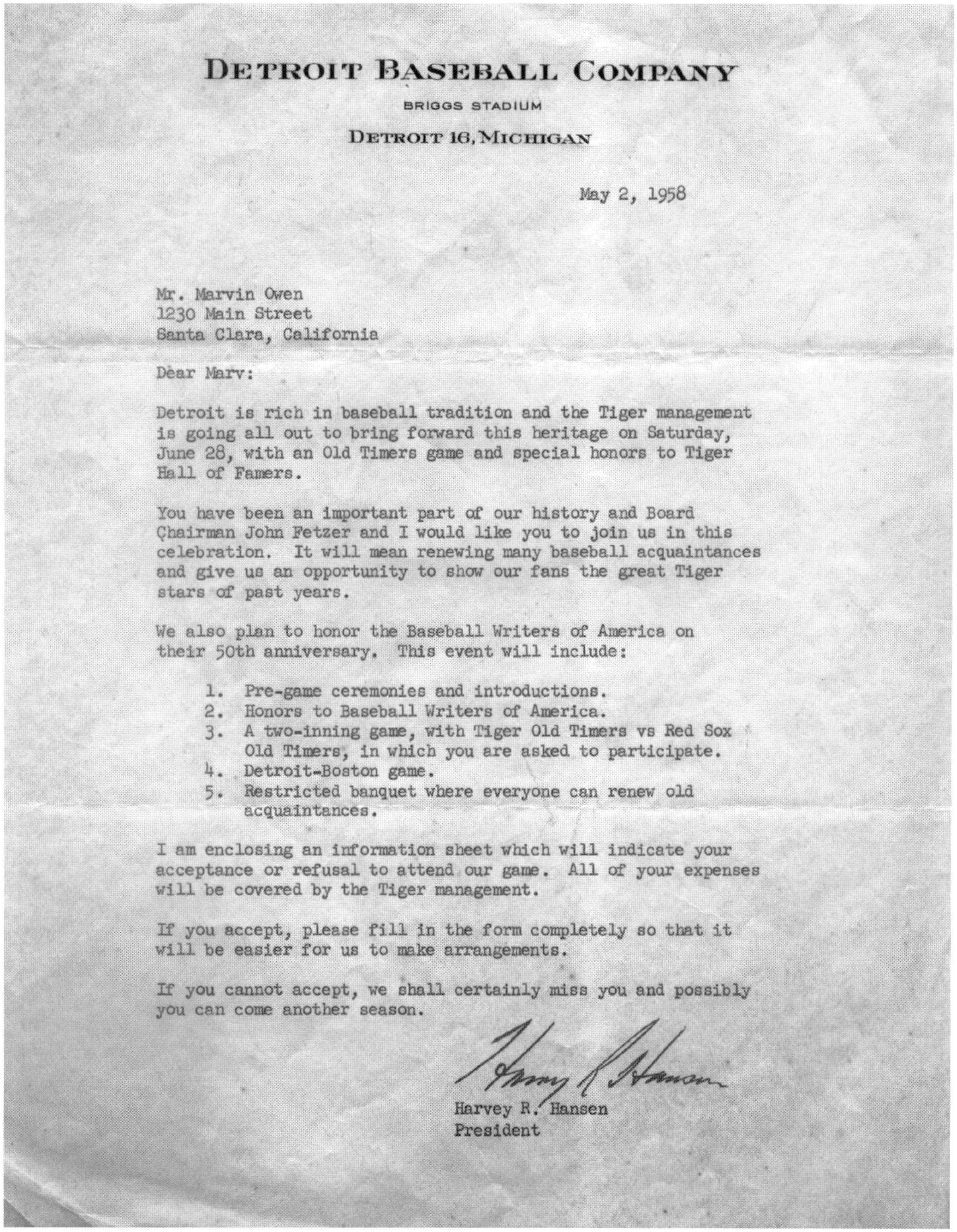

DETROIT BASEBALL COMPANY

BRIGGS STADIUM

DETROIT 16, MICHIGAN

May 2, 1958

Mr. Marvin Owen
1230 Main Street
Santa Clara, California

Dear Marv:

Detroit is rich in baseball tradition and the Tiger management is going all out to bring forward this heritage on Saturday, June 28, with an Old Timers game and special honors to Tiger Hall of Famers.

You have been an important part of our history and Board Chairman John Fetzer and I would like you to join us in this celebration. It will mean renewing many baseball acquaintances and give us an opportunity to show our fans the great Tiger stars of past years.

We also plan to honor the Baseball Writers of America on their 50th anniversary. This event will include:

1. Pre-game ceremonies and introductions.
2. Honors to Baseball Writers of America.
3. A two-inning game, with Tiger Old Timers vs Red Sox Old Timers, in which you are asked to participate.
4. Detroit-Boston game.
5. Restricted banquet where everyone can renew old acquaintances.

I am enclosing an information sheet which will indicate your acceptance or refusal to attend our game. All of your expenses will be covered by the Tiger management.

If you accept, please fill in the form completely so that it will be easier for us to make arrangements.

If you cannot accept, we shall certainly miss you and possibly you can come another season.

Harvey R. Hansen
President

117

Napoleon "Nap" Lajoie
(from Touching Second, 1910 the Reilly and Britton Co.)

The 1934 plywood tiger always had a place of honor in my mother's home. It sat on top of the Majestic radio console. On the front of the tiger was signed Babe Ruth and on the other side was signed Heinie Schuble, Rudy York, Gerry Walker, Mickey Cochrane, Marvin Owen, Schoolboy Rowe, Eldon Auker, Chief Hogsett, Billy Rogell, Chas. Gehringer, Jo-Jo White, Pete Fox, Gen Crowder, Cy Perkins, Ray Hayworth and others whose names have faded. In later years a baseball collector said it was probably worth hundreds of dollars even in its faded condition. In the October 1989 Loma Prieta earthquake, the tiger fell and broke into several pieces. But not to worry, a restoration specialist put it back together perfectly at a cost of over 100 dollars.

When I heard that it had been put back together at great cost, I really laughed. "Those signatures are not authentic! A clubhouse boy in 1934 was very good at replicating signatures and he did them all. Sorry."

Once as a scout for Detroit, I was watching the American Legion game and the pitcher was yanked. I saw the relief chucker, a lefthander, throw four pitches. Then I turned to a friend for a few minutes of conversation. When I looked out to the mound again, I said to my other friend, "Why did they replace the lefthander with a righthander?" All my friend said was, "Same kid." He was ambidextrous.

I liked to challenge myself or others, to games of recall. One of my favorites was listing by memory Hall of Fame players and their year of selection. Another recall game I liked was recalling baseball players' nicknames. Nicknames that were often bantered around randomly were: Bush, Big Bush, Little Bush, Meat, Meathead, Showboat, Efus and RA among others.

These nicknames for certain players quickly came to mind:

Herman Clinton, **Flea**
Mickey Cochrane, **Black Mike**
Alvin Crowder, **General**
Jay Dean, **Dizzy**
Paul Dean, **Daffy**
Dom DiMaggio, **Little Professor**
Joe DiMaggio, **The Yankee Clipper**
Bob Feller, **Rapid Robert**
Earvin Fox, **Pete**
Jimmy Foxx **The Beast**
Lou Gehrig, **The Iron Horse**
Charlie Gehringer, **Chollie, The Mechanical Man and The Champ**
Leon Goslin, **Goose**
Henry Greenberg, **Hank**
Mike Higgins, **Pinky**
Walter Johnson, **The Big Train**
John Martin, **Pepper**
Joe Medwick, **Ducky**
Marvin Owen, **Freck, Steak**
William Rogell, **Billy**
Lynwood Rowe, **Schoolboy**
Harold Ruel, **Muddy**
George Herman Ruth, **Babe, The Sultan of Swat**
George Tebbetts, **Birdie**
Gerald Walker, **Gee**
Lloyd Waner, **Little Poison**
Paul Waner, **Big Poison**
Joyner White, **Jo-Jo**
Then, of course, there were the "Lefty's":
Vernon Gomez, **Lefty**
Robert Grove, **Lefty**
Francis O'Doul, **Lefty**

If I were to list my candidates for a Dream Team, here it is:

- "For managers, let's start off with Connie Mack and John McGraw.
- Mickey Cochrane was the best catcher I ever saw; he could catch, throw, hit, run and besides that he could get you to play your very best. He helped my hitting ability; he could give us pep talks to keep us winning. I'd like Yogi Berra to catch, too.
- At first base give me Lou Gehrig and George Sisler.
- Charlie Gehringer was the best second sacker I ever saw. I'd also like Nap Lajoie and Eddie Collins.
- At third base I'd like Pinky Higgins and Jimmy Collins.
- At shortstop let's have Honus Wagner and Joe Cronin.

Honus Wagner
(from Touching Second, 1910 the Reilly and Britton Co.)

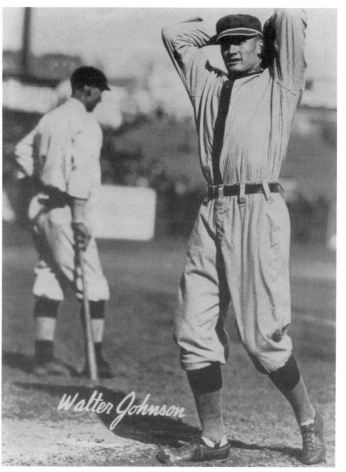

Walter Johnson — Washington Senators
"The Big Train"
(Thanks to: Rev. Jerome C. Romanowski, Holy Name Society)

- In the outfield I'd have Cobb, Ruth, DiMaggio, Doc Cramer, Goose Goslin, Tris Speaker.
- To give us strength in pitching there would be Walter Johnson, Dizzy Dean, Fred Hutchison, Cy Young, Lefty Grove, Bob Feller.

How about that?"

Eddie Collins
(from Touching Second, 1910 the Reilly and Britton Co.)

Ty Cobb
(from Touching Second, 1910 the Reilly and Britton Co.)

119

Babe Ruth Display
Cooperstown, N.Y.
(National Baseball Library and Archive, Cooperstown, N.Y.)

Reminiscing

There was a famous ball player, Ruth, star with the Yankees
Playing pro ball for him was enjoyment and a breeze.
One of his teammates a great hitter, Lou Gehrig,
He was no runt, was a guy very strong and big.

The shortstop was a good one, Frankie Crosetti.
On the field and at bat he was always ready.
Behind the bat was a Hall of Famer, Billy Dickey.
Played before Hall of Famer Mantle Mickey.

In c f, at late stage of Ruth's career was Joe Di Maggio
Ability of a real star and always gave a good show.
On pitching staff were Gomez and Ruffing
They both with velocity could throw that thing.

Joe Sewell, ex Cleveland ss, for NY, played 3rd.
Could get ball to 1st base as fast as a bird.
At 2nd was Californian Tony Lazzeri
When he came to bat all Yank fans would become so merry.

When Ruth came to bat in Yankee Stadium,
fans would yell, "We want a home run."
Then, by golly, he would step right up to
the plate and he'd hit one!
Later there were others: Aaron, Greenberg, Mays, McCovey,
Kiner, Williams and Mantle.
Regarding Babe Ruth, to him none could hold a candle.
Babe Ruth was the greatest, that is my view.
Until it's disproven I'll believe it is true.

M.O.

Babe Ruth   Knute Rockne   Lou Gehrig

This is the picture that hung in Marv's livingroom.

(On the back Marv wrote: Ruth: he and Cobb were the outstanding players. The best of the lot.

Knute Rockne: outstanding football coach of Notre Dame University.

Lou Gehrig: outstanding 1st sacker, Yanks, hit 2136 consecutive games in American League.)

From my earliest days of baseball, I always thought Babe Ruth was the greatest and I looked up to him as my hero. The first time I saw him in person was in San Jose in 1928 when he and Lou Gehrig played an exhibition game at Sodality Field, but I was too shy to speak to either man. In 1933 when I was a rookie playing for Detroit, Babe Ruth passed me on the field and said, "Hi there, kid." He called everyone kid. That was a great thrill. We all loved him, too, because if he got a raise, then it was easier for us to get one too! Six years later at the Cooperstown Baseball Centennial Celebration Babe signed a ball for me as one of the eleven charter Hall of Fame members. After I retired, I kept a framed photograph of Babe Ruth, Lou Gehrig, and Knute Rockne hanging in a place of honor in my home. I always said, "Ruth is the greatest ball player I've ever seen."

A young Babe Ruth probably 1921

The Best

The best ball players I have seen
If all were on one team
Would be a beautiful scene
Start with Babe Ruth, the Sultan of Swat
He was the greatest of the lot.

The Yankee Clipper Joe Di Maggio
He was one of the best in the big show.

Second base star Gehringer could run, throw, hit, field
To no other player did he ever have to yield.

Lefty Grove, pitcher I faced on the mound
He was the best in any state, city or town.

Great catcher was Mickey Cochrane.
He could throw, field, hit and run.
Winning with him was a lot of fun.

Another catching star, super player could do it all, Cub Gabby Harnett
To steal a base off him was just impossible to get.

Good fast ball and curve ball too, Bobby Feller, Cleveland Indian
Had too much stuff, batting against him was no fun.

A great pitcher Giant Carl Hubbell
When the game started, he gave all hitters hell.

Jimmy Foxx, Pride of the Philadelphia A's
With both bat and glove had outstanding days.

A Tiger star was Greenberg, Hank
With the bat the baseball he could spank.

Red Ruffing starting pitcher there was no doubt.
Had little difficulty getting hitters out.

This is just the beginning of a super star team
Enough to make any manager beam.
                                        M.O.

Along the way Marv met many interesting, helpful and famous people. When asked to name a few he thought a while and remembered.

"Once when I was coming back to the Detroit dugout I passed Lou Gehrig of the New York Yankees and he said, 'Marv, that was the best catch I've ever seen.' Naturally that made me feel good for a week! It was almost as good as when Babe Ruth said, 'Hi Kid' to me.

Babe Ruth was the greatest Yankee of 'em all
He could deliver the home run ball.
Second greatest Yankee was 1st sacker Lou Gehrig.
Look out pitcher when his spikes he would dig
He's getting prepared to hit the ball over the fence.
Walk him, pitcher, if you have any sense.

He was the greatest Tiger of 'em all - Ty Cobb
Great hitter, every base he would rob.

Second greatest Tiger was Gehringer by far.
Good hitter, good runner and fielder all star.
Quiet Charlie never said much when playing ball.
His big bat and sure-fire glove said it all.

M.O.

As I look back I think of all the sports writers who were writing when I was beginning my career and how they are remembered as great writers in their fields: Bob Considine, James Reston, Grantland Rice, Damon Runyan, H.G. Salsinger and Bud Shaver. I have saved many of their sports articles from the thirties.

Of course, I have to mention Joe Louis as a notable along the way. He and I both felt a loyalty to Detroit and I felt the people of Detroit gave me a lot of support. I think Joe felt that way too. Joe was a good friend."

(Source: National Baseball Library and Archive, Cooperstown, N.Y.)

Many years later, the famous world heavyweight champion, Joe Louis, came to San Jose and Buddy Leitch of the San Jose Evening News ran this story:

"Asked For Owen...

WHEN ASKED if he was going to specialize on perfecting any one punch for his title defense, Joe replied:

'I think not; after all I have only two hands and with those hands I can deliver just so many punches.... After all, there are no new punches. It's how the punch is delivered that counts.... That's true of everything.... It's not the notes in music, it's how they are played.'

With one exception, Louis was highly pleased with his San Jose visit.... He attracted a capacity crowd, his work as referee was well received and he knocked down a nice hunk of cash.... But he was disappointed in visiting Marv Owen's home town and finding Owen out of town.

Louis - Sharkey Fight, 1935, Yankee Stadium, N.Y.
(UPI/Bettmann)

'Where's my favorite third baseman?' was the first question he asked.... 'That Owen, when playing for Detroit, gave me some of my greatest thrills, especially when he came tearing in for a bunt, fielded the ball with his bare hand and made the throw to first all in one move.... He could make that play better than any third sacker in history,' Joe stated. What do you mean, he COULD.... He still can—and does."

John J. McHale who in the 1950's (1951 through 1956) was the Tiger's Assistant Farm Director and Farm Director and then, (in 1957) became the Detroit Tigers General Manager. In 1952 until 1954 Marv managed three Detroit farm clubs: Davenport, Durham and Valdosta. In 1954 Marv moved into the Tiger scouting department. Marv and John (later President of the Montreal Expos) kept in touch and corresponded for over 40 years.

When the University of Santa Clara Baseball Yearbook was published in 1983, it was John J. McHale who wrote the dedication.

"DEDICATION

The 1983 Santa Clara Baseball Yearbook is dedicated with great affection to one of the great names in Bronco diamond history, MARV OWEN.

Over the years, Santa Clara has nurtured a superb baseball tradition with 38 former players advancing to the major leagues. None were more capable than Marv. A member of the Class of 1930, he made the transition from a college first baseman to one of the best defensive third basemen in the major leagues.

One year after his graduation, Marv played in the majors with the Detroit Tigers. After a year in the minor leagues he returned for good in 1933 and became part of one of the top infields in the league with Billy Rogell at short, Charley Gehringer at second and Hank Greenberg at first. He was a member of the Tigers from 1933-37, the Chicago White Sox in 1938-39, and the Boston Red Sox in 1940. He played in the 1934 and 1935 World Series, distinguishing himself in both.

Following his playing career he managed in the Tiger and Red Sox organizations for several seasons before becoming a full-time scout with Detroit. He held that post until his retirement several years ago.

Marv is still active with Bronco baseball. It is seldom that he ever misses a home game, and is still sought out for help by players and coaches alike. His baseball knowledge and loyalty to Santa Clara is invaluable.

The following is a letter received in the athletic department commenting on his dedication.

'Your decision to dedicate the 1983 baseball season in honor of Marv Owen is applauded by all his many friends. It has been my good fortune to have been acquainted with such a fine player, associate, and friend for the past 40 years. Marv was a great athlete dedicated to professional excellence. He was always committed to Santa Clara and wore its colors well.'

John J. McHale, President
Montreal Expos Baseball Club"

Credit:: University of Santa Clara

126

Here is a letter I have saved since 1976 and a picture from John J. McHale, former President of the Montreal Expos dated Jan. 13, 1976.

expos

office of the president

January 13th, 1976

Mr. Marvin Owen, Scout
c/o Detroit Tigers Baseball Club
Tiger Stadium
Detroit, Mich. 48216

Dear Marvin:

Patty and I always enjoy your very thoughtful Christmas gift.
The older I get, the more I appreciate God's natural gifts.

Last spring I went to the White House with Joe Cronin and
Bowie Kuhn to present President Ford with his gold baseball
pass. The President is a good sports fan and was a super
football player at Michigan in 1934 and 1935.

In the course of reminiscing, he said, where is Marvin Owen?
This gave me a chance to say something authoritatively. Of
course, we then went through the Joe Medwick affair, scouting
for Detroit etc.

Thought you would like to know this.

Best in 1976.

Sincerely,

John J. McHale
President

JJM:sb

Left to right: John McHale, Pres. Montreal Ball Club, Bowie Kuhn, Baseball Commissioner, President Gerald Ford, Joe Cronin, Hall of Fame Ball Player, President of American League. (1975)

(Thanks to Former President Gerald Ford and John McHale)

Because the photo was taken at the White House, a letter was written asking permission from former President Ford. That letter and President Ford's reply follow.

August 15, 1993
Former President Gerald Ford
c/o Judy Rish
P. O. Box 927
Rancho Mirage, CA 92262

Dear President Ford,

Five years ago before my brother Marv Owen, 3rd sacker for the Detroit Tigers in the '30's, died he and I began writing a book, describing his baseball career. Among the pictures we wished to use in the publication was the one of you, Joe Cronin, John McHale and Bowie Kuhn. John sent the picture to my brother with an accompanying letter indicating that you had asked at that time, "Where is Marv Owen?" and that a baseball discussion followed.

I wrote to John McHale for permission to publish the picture in the book and he saw no problem. However, I would appreciate your written permission to include the photo in the publication.

Thank you for your help. If you have questions, please call me at (408) 688-4801. A copy of the picture is enclosed.

Sincerely,
Vi Owen

P.S. We share a common problem; I had a knee replacement last year. I'd like to know more about the knee surgery you had.

GERALD R. FORD

August 31, 1993

Dear Ms. Owen:

I gladly authorize the use of the photo of Joe Cronin, John McHale, Bowie Kuhn and me in the publication of a book of Marv Owen - his autobiography.

I'm still a dedicated Tiger fan and have great recollections of the fine career of Marv.

I've had two total knee joint replacements. Left knee - 1990. Right knee - 1992. Both very successful. Hope you had the same good results.

Best regards,

Gerald R. Ford

Ms. Viola Owen
Aptos, California   95003

DETROIT BASEBALL COMPANY

DETROIT, MICHIGAN 48216 TELEPHONE 962-4000

James A. Campbell
President
General Manager
November 17, 1982

Dear Marv:

Forgive me for not having written to you sooner about the retirement of Charlie Gehringer's and Hank Greenberg's numbers. Lord only knows, you have been pressing me to do this for years and I finally took your advice!

Really, Marv, I think both fellows were delighted to learn that we were going to file Number 2 and Number 5. These two fellows were not only great ballplayers, but as you and I well know, they are two of the finest gentlemen I have ever had the opportunity to know. I wasn't around here when they were playing, but from what I could observe in later years, you fellows had a lot of class on that ball club. I didn't get to know all of those fellows, but I did get to know Mickey, Hank, Charlie, Billy, Schoolboy, Tommy and a few others, and, oh yes, even my old pal Marv Owen (really top drawer!).

Seriously, Marv, I was just ten and eleven years old when you fellows were winning in '34 and '35. I lived down in Ohio on Lake Erie, right between Toledo and Cleveland, and we could pick up the Detroit games on radio coming across the lake much better than we could the Cleveland broadcasts. I really think the interest that I developed in the Detroit team started a little fire that smoldered for another fifteen years while I won World War II, finished college, and then got a job working for the Tigers in Thomasville, Georgia. Its all been great ever since!

We plan on inviting Charlie's and Hank's teammates to join us the weekend that we retire those numbers so keep yourself free around the 12th of June. We'll be sending you more information later on. I might even let you sing the National Anthem!

All the best wishes for the Holiday Season.

Regards,
Jim

As far as Marv was concerned Chollie was one of the greatest ball players who ever played in the majors! To prove his point in a 1980 letter to Jim Campbell, Tigers General Manager, he presented these Gehringer stats:

Years	Hits	2b	3b	HR	RBI	SO	SB	BB	BA	Runs
19	2839	574	146	184	1427	372	181	1186	320	1774

In yearly averages the stats were:

BB	Hits	RBI
62.3	149.4	75.1

He used these stats in presenting his case to honor Chollie by having the Detroit Tiger organization retire uniform "2".

Again in 1981 Marv wrote to Jim Campbell, President & General Manager urging retirement of Chollie's uniform and number. (The Owen family is persistent. One of us is nicknamed "Water on the Rock!")

On November 17, 1982, Marv received a letter from Jim Campbell, President and General Manager.

REMEMBERING CHARLIE GEHRINGER AND HANK GREENBERG Retiring Number 2 and Number 5

*Autographed ball by
Charlie Gehringer*

The following correspondence was sent in preparation for the Charlie and Hank uniform numbers retirement ceremony.

DETROIT BASEBALL COMPANY

DETROIT, MICHIGAN 48216 TELEPHONE 962-4000

April 25, 1983
Mr. Marvin Owen
42 Hawthorne Way
San Jose, CA 95110

Dear Marv:

We thank you for accepting to join us at the Gehringer-Greenberg Day on Sunday, June 12. We all anticipate an exciting time.

Briefly, here is what we have planned for you. Within the next two weeks, you will receive a check covering the cost of round trip airline ticket for you. The check should cover round-trip transportation. If the check is insufficient, we will reimburse the difference upon presentation of airline voucher. A reservation has been secured in your name at the Westin Hotel in downtown Detroit for the night of Saturday, June 11. If you plan to spend Sunday evening, June 12 in Detroit, you must call Lew Matlin (313) 962-4000 by May 13.

A dinner has been planned for all returning members of the 1934, 35 and 40 teams for Saturday evening at the Detroit Athletic Club. Bus transportation will be provided for the Westin Hotel. A Sunday brunch from 11 to 12-noon has been planned for in the hotel. The media will be invited to the brunch. Bus transportation to the park will be provided at 12:30 p.m. The doubleheader is scheduled to start at 1:30 p.m. with ceremonies between games. Bus transportation back to the hotel will be available immediately after the second game.

Incidental expenses incurred during your stay should be sent to William E. Haase, Vice-president/Operations, Tiger Stadium, Detroit, MI 48216 upon your return home.

Further information will be forthcoming. Should you have any questions, please direct them to Lew Matlin. Thanks for your support.

Sincerely,

Dan Ewald
Public Relations Director
DE:rg

DETROIT BASEBALL CLUB
DEPARTMENTAL COMMUNICATION

VERBAL ORDERS DON'T GO

FROM   Lew Matlin
TO   All Concerned   DATE 6/9/83
SUBJECT   GEHRINGER-GREENBERG DAY
          CAR PAIRINGS

1. Elden Auker from Vero Beach, FL
    Herman "Flea" Clifton from Cincinnati, OH

2. Ray Hayworth from High Point, NY
    Elon "Chief" Hogsett from Hays, KS

3. Marv Owen from San Jose, CA
    Billy Rogell from New Port Richey, FL

4. Heinie Schuble from Baytown, TX
    Joe Sullivan from Sequim, WA

5. Joyner "Jo Jo" White from Tacoma, WA
    Dick Bartell from Alameda, CA

6. Barney McCosky from Vero Beach, FL
    L. D. "Dutch" Meyer from Forth Worth, TX

7. Hal Newhouser from Bloomfield Hills, MI
    Tom Seats from San Francisco, CA

8. Clay Smith from Cambridge, KS
    George "Tuck" Stainback from Newbury Park, CA

9. Billy Sullivan from Sarasota, FL
    George "Birdie" Tibbetts from Anna Marie, FL

10. Charles Gehringer from Birmingham, MI
    Hank Greenberg from Beverly Hills, CA

DETROIT BASEBALL CLUB
DEPARTMENTAL COMMUNICATION

VERBAL ORDERS DON'T GO   DATE   6/10/83

FROM   Lew Matlin   Dan Ewald

TO   Bill Freehan   Al Kaline
       Vince Desmond   Ernie Harwell
       George Kell   Vic Wertz
       Fred Smith

SUBJECT   GEHRINGER-GREENBERG
       CEREMONY

Attached, please find diagrams highlighting the field program.

Please meet Vince Desmond in the Tiger Dugout at the conclusion of the first game.

You will take your slot in front of the pitcher's mound after the last invitee is seated.

Ernie Harwell will open program and he will ask Vic Wertz and Bill Freehan to alternate presenting souvenir bats per attached diagram.

George Kell will present door stop to Hank Greenberg.

Al Kaline will present door stop to Charlie Gehringer.

Vic Wertz presents framed original poster art to Hank Greenberg.

Bill Freehan presents framed original poster art to Charlie Gehringer.

Al Kaline "retires" Charlie Gehringer's uniform #2. (Brief remarks).

Response by Mr. Gehringer.

George Kell "retires" Hank Greenberg's uniform #5. (Brief response).

Response by Mr. Greenberg.

Mr. Harwell closes ceremony.

Vince Desmond will lead the program participants off the field.

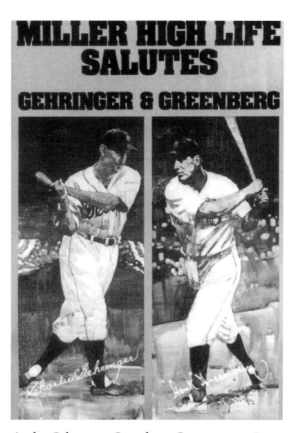

At the Gehringer-Greenberg Ceremony on June 12, 1983 a poster, 20" x 38" commemorating the occasion was given as a souvenir. Retiring #2 & #5

GEHRINGER-GREENBERG DAY
Sunday, June 12, 1983
SEATING AREA CHART

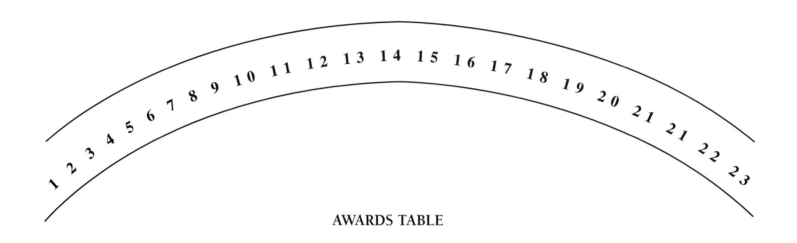

AWARDS TABLE

ERNIE HARWELL - MASTER OF CEREMONIES`

1. Auker	9. White	17. McCosky
2. Clifton	10. Kell	18. Meyer
3. Hayworth	11. Wertz	19. Newhouser
4. Hogsett	12. Greenberg	20. Smith
5. Owen	13. Gehringer	21. Stainback
6. Rogell	14. Freehan	22. B. Sullivan
7. Schuble	15. Kaline	23. Tebbetts
8. J. Sullivan	16. Bartell	

GEHRINGER-GREENBERG DAY
Sunday, June 12, 1983

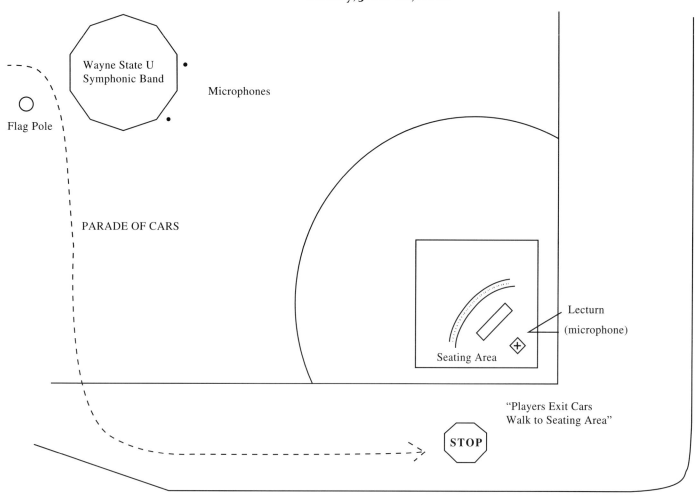

Car #1	Elden Auker - Herman Clifton	Car #6	Barney McCosky - Dutch Meyer
Car #2	Ray Hayworth - Elon Hogsett	Car #7	Hal Newhouser - Tom Seats
Car #3	Marvin Owen - Bill Rogell	Car #8	Clay Smith - George Stainback
Car #4	Heinie Schuble - Joe Sullivan	Car #9	Billy Sullivan - George Tebbetts
Car #5	JoJo White - Dick Bartell	Car #10	Charles Gehringer - Hank Greenberg

Autographed ball by Charlie Gehringer Mechanical Man — a nickname given Charlie by Lefty Gomez

Billy Rogell and Marv Owen
June 12, 1983

(Thanks to Mrs. Chas. L. Gehringer)

Marv was happy that Charlie and Hank were honored at the ceremony. The four members of the "Infield of Dreams"— Greenberg, Gehringer, Rogell and Owen remembered the old days and then caught up on what each had been doing for the last 46 years:Hank Greenberg, a baseball executive and stock market investor; Charlie Gehringer, a Detroit business man; Billy Rogell, a Detroit Councilman; and Marv Owen, a California real estate investor, all successful in their new careers after baseball.

Commemorative bat

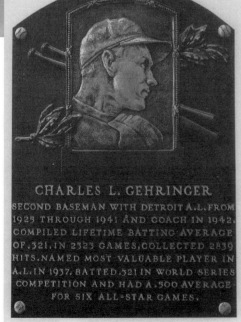

The June 12, 1983, ceremony was a fitting tribute to the two Hall of Fame members, Charlie Gehringer and Hank Greenberg.

(National Baseball Library and Archive, Cooperstown, N.Y.)

Marv in his eighties

I came with freckles on my face.
Now old age has slowed my pace.

Time goes fast.
Money goes fast.
Planes go fast.
Age goes fast.
Happiness goes fast -
old age creeps upon us quickly.
Enjoyable times go fast.
How come things that we want to go slowly, naturally go quickly,
but situations that we want to go quickly
just snailpace and go slowly?

All the oldtime newspaper comics are gone.
New comics, look at 'em, they make me yawn.
Used to be Happy Hooligan, Jiggs and Katzenjammer Kids.
All were eliminated, must have hit the skids.
Some other oldtime comics were discontinued too.
Today some are very bush league even if they are new.

Yesterday evening at four after five
Scared as hell but glad to be alive
A large shock hit, a big earthquake
And wow did my house quiver and shake!
All my life have been through many earthquakes
But this one really gave me the scary shakes.
The quake just shook and shook and shook.
All my fearlessness the earthquake took.

After dinner it's easy to fall asleep in an easy chair -
I do it many a day.
Guess that is what goes with old age -
that is what many do say.

No doubt, that is why I'm club president today
And our Senile Club student body grows day by day.
As long as time exists, Senile Club will be here, too.
So see, we are only a small part of it, me and you.

We for centuries have been trying to figure out what is life?
'Tis a combination of happiness and strife.
When the latter hits us it seems so strong.
What we want is more happiness, that's where we belong.
But we don't have too much choice in that direction
For at anytime strife may step in and ruin our selection.
Sickness is a part of strife.
It's certainly a part of life.
There is nothing we can do about it,
Just bear down and hope to re-route it.

As you say, days do go faster,
But old age makes me go slower.
As young man I was thinner,
but as old man I am heavier.
As young man had auburn colored hair
As old man it is now grayish white.
As young man had quickness and bounce.
As old man losing my pep by the ounce.
As young man never thought I'd be a Senile Member
Now with old age have trouble trying to remember.
I remember without a puff, I could dash around the bases.
Now at my age, I'm all in when I pick up two 7-up 6 pack cases.

I came with Freckles on my face.
Now old age has slowed my pace.

M.O.

IV. TIGER TRACKS—
MEMORIES AND MEMORABILIA

Marv saved memories of his baseball life through his memorabilia. These pages show you some of the things he saved. He called his memorabilia book his "fathead book."

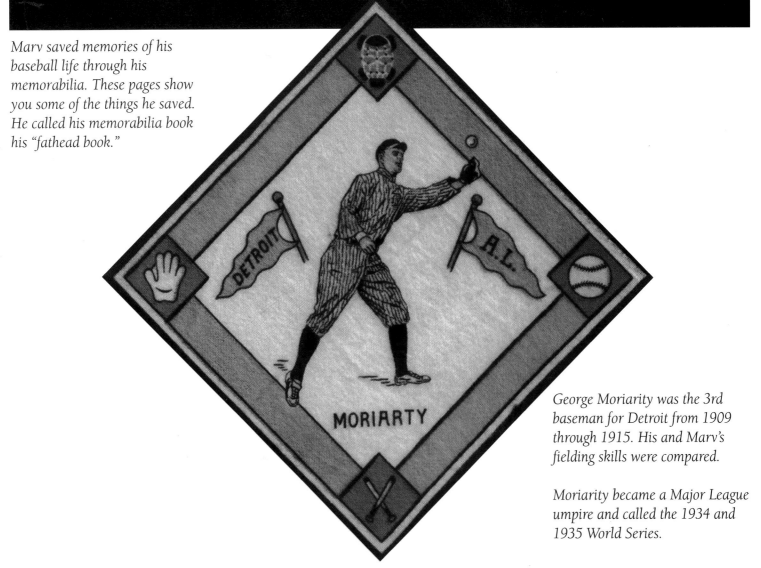

MORIARTY

George Moriarity was the 3rd baseman for Detroit from 1909 through 1915. His and Marv's fielding skills were compared.

Moriarity became a Major League umpire and called the 1934 and 1935 World Series.

137

Marvin Owen

MARVIN JAMES OWEN,
SENSATIONAL TIGER THIRD
BASEMAN—WAS BORN IN SAN-
JOSE, CALIFORNIA, MARCH 2,
1908~ATTENDED SANTA CLARA
UNIVERSITY—JOINED THE
TIGERS IN 1931~SENT AWAY
FOR MORE EXPERIENCE—
STARRED AS A MEMBER OF
NEWARK~VOTED THE MOST
VALUABLE PLAYER IN THE
INTERNATIONAL LEAGUE
IN 1932—

WHEN MARVIN'S PLAYING DAYS
ARE OVER, HE INTENDS TO GO BACK
TO SAN JOSE AND TEACH SCHOOL~

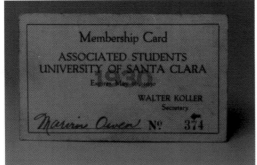

Marv's University of Santa Clara Student
Body Card 1930 Senior Year.....

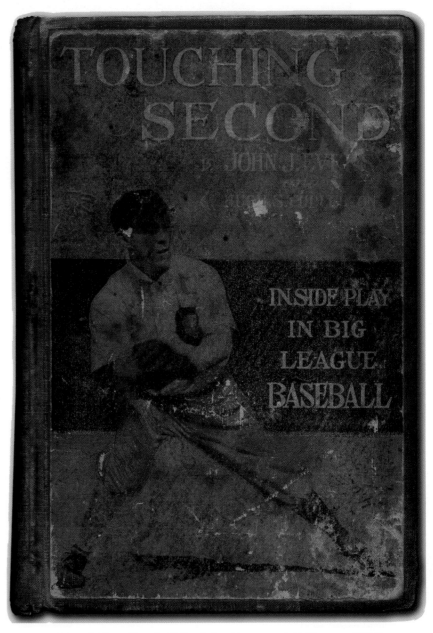

Marv's First Baseball Book by Evers and Fullerton, 1910

Marv's Detroit Baseball Cap

Detroit Baseball Club Trunk Tag

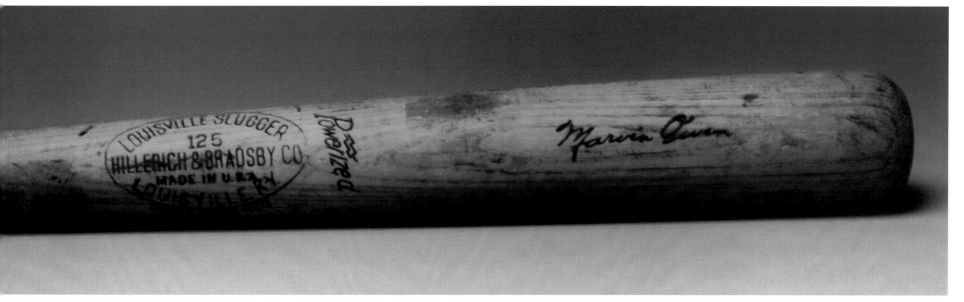

Marvin Owen Louisville Slugger Bat

139

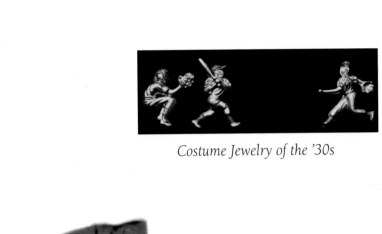

Costume Jewelry of the '30s

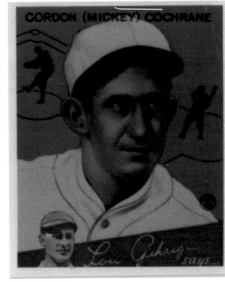

GORDON (MICKEY) COCHRANE

A Great Catcher/Manager

Wooden Tiger with Names of 1934 Detroit Team Members
This was the "autographed" tiger damaged in the 1989 Loma Prieta Earthquake. It was restored at great expense.

Among the best!

Autographed Baseball with 1934 Detroit Team members
— 24 signatures

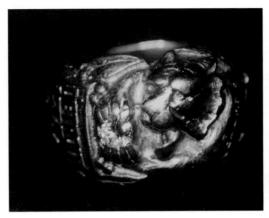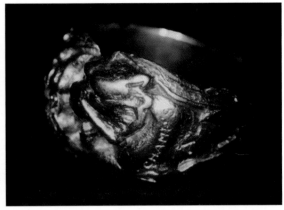

1934 Championship Ring

(Photo credit: Roger Sita, WA)

1931 Acquired by Detroit Tigers
Detroit 3rd Baseman

DIAMOND STARS, No. 67

Marvin Owen, Detroit's third baseman, is a good example of quick, cat-like action in a position where batted balls often travel like a white streak with little time to play the bounces cleanly. Third base, called the "red light" spot, by reason of the danger of line drives and whistling grounders, is one where fast footwork and lightning movement is essential. Hits that are blocked with the glove or body can usually be recovered in time to make the putout at first. Due to bunts and the fact that a third baseman often has to "blindly" play on a base runner who approaches from his back, makes it the hardest job in the infield to play with finesse.

MARVIN J. OWEN. Born San Jose, Calif., 27 years old; bats and throws right; 6 ft. 1 inch, 177 pounds. Hit for .317 in 1934, .069 World Series. One of 240 major league players with playing tips. ©1935 National Chicle Co. Cambridge, Mass. U.S.A.

1935 Diamond Stars Card #67

Navin Field

142

Marvin Owen Louisville Slugger
Miniature Bat

1934-5 DETROIT TIGERS

Marv Owen   3B

Marv Owen Appointed Deputy Sheriff of Santa
Clara County after 1935 World Series

Marv Owen

Marvin Owen Baseball
Card

159 Marv Owen

3rd base

Played 9 years in the big leagues, begining in 1931 with the Tigers. Collected 179 hits with 96 R.B.I's and a .317 batting average in 1934, as Detroit won the pennant. Drove in 105 runs while batting .295 in 1936. After hitting .288 in 1937, Marv went to the White Sox the following year, where he gathered 162 hits for a .281 average. Spent his final year in 1940 with the Red Sox. Played every infield position during his career. Had 1040 hits for a .275 lifetime batting average.

GRAND SLAM 1978

Autographed Ball Signed by the Eleven Hall of Famers at Cooperstown, June 12, 1939

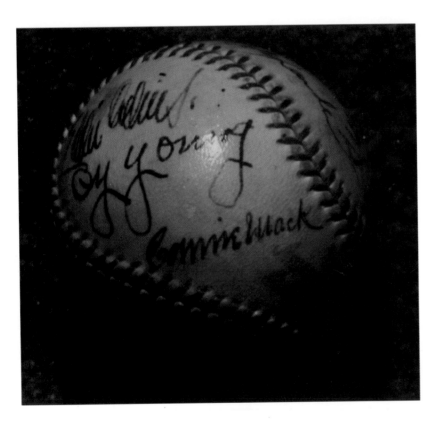

Eddie Collins
Cy Young
Connie Mack

Ty Cobb
Babe Ruth
Honus Wagner

Grover Alexander
George Sisler
Walter Johnson

Tris Speaker
Napoleon Lajoie (not visable on side)

145

Marv is traded to the Boston Red Sox.
1940 (Trunk Tag)

One of Charlie Gehringer's
Business Ventures

1937 American League Schedule

50th Anniversary of the
National Association of
Professional Baseball
Leagues, 1951

Batter Up #168
1935, Marv Owen Card

Marv is traded to the
Chicago White Sox, 1938.

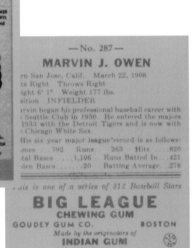

Heads Up #287
Marv Owen Card

Marv manages and plays third for
Portland Beavers, Pacific Coast League.
Wins the League Pennant, 1945.

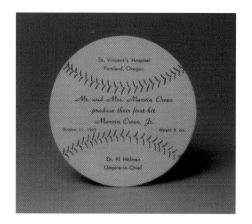

Marvin Owen, Jr. is born
October 11, 1945.

Manages the San Jose Red Sox
1947 through 1951.

1944 Portland Schedule

*Lakeland Florida
Celebrates the Silver
Anniversary of Detroit
Tigers 1934 World
Series - 1959*

*Game Tickets
San Jose Red Sox
opening night 1949*

*Marv joins Detroit Tigers Organization
Scouting Department, 1954.*

*Manages the Durham Bulls
1953*

Schedule and Roster

Marv volunteers at the University of Santa Clara. Shown with the late Sal Taormina, Santa Clara University, Baseball Coach.

Commemorative Bottle: Baseball's 100th Anniversary 1969

Marv designs a Louisville slugger bat that commemorates the World Record of 462 RBIs of the 1934 Detroit Infield. He presents a commemorative bat to Hank Greenberg, Charlie Gehringer and Billy Rogell - 1984.

Santa Clara Valley Hall of Fame Plaque
Awarded to Marv Owen, 1968

BELLARMINE ATHLETIC HALL OF FAME
1972
MARVIN OWEN
DETROIT TIGERS, CHICAGO WHITE SOX,
BOSTON RED SOX – WORLD SERIES 1934-1935

Bellarmine Hall of Fame Plaque Presented to Marv in 1972

Marv Enjoys Retirement

Marv's Sister, Babe, Mother and Son, Skip
(Marv Owen, Jr.) 1974

"Charlie", 1991
(*Thanks to Mrs. Chas. L. Gehringer*)

Commemorative Glass
Detroit Tigers
1968 World Series

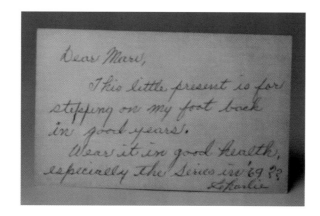

Card Accompanying Gift from Charlie Gehringer
to Marv After
1968 World Series

Marvin Owen
San Jose - Calif.

Portrait of Marv by an
artist in the '30s

152

The 1934 Detroit Tigers World Series uniform consisting of pants, shirt, cap and socks, all in A-1 condition, was a most treasured possession that Marv kept neatly placed in boxes complete with mothballs from 1934 to 1988, fifty-four years. After much careful thought, on Feb. 29, 1988 he donated it all to the Domino's Pizza Foundation to be a part of the Detroit Tigers Archives and Museum.

In the spring of 1993 the search was on for the 1934 World Series Uniform. Domino Pizza was no longer the owner of the Detroit Tigers, the team had been sold to Little Caesar's Pizza. Through various phone calls and the following correspondence the missing uniform was found.

May 12, 1993
Ms. Alice Sloane
Detroit Tigers Baseball Club
Tiger Stadium
Detroit, Michigan 48216

Dear Alice,
Thank you for helping me on the phone. I appreciate your assistance.
I called Betsy at Domino Pizza to ask what had happened to two items that my brother, Marv Owen, had donated to the Domino Pizza Foundation in 1988 for its Detroit Tigers Archives and Museum (which is no more). She told me that the two items: 1) Major League record bat (RBIs), and 2) the 1934 World Series Detroit Uniform (pants, shirt, cap and socks all in A-1 condition) had been given to the new Tiger owners organization. Will you see if you can find out for me where these items are and what is to become of them? My brother really valued these for their meaning to him.
Thank you again for your help.
Sincerely,
Vi Owen

Detroit Tigers
TIGER STADIUM · DETROIT, MICHIGAN 48216 · (313) 962-4000

June 21, 1993

Dear Vi:
I don't know if Alice Sloane had an opportunity to call you with the whereabouts of your brother's bat and uniform. If not, please be advised that they are securely included in our Corporate Archives at Little Caesar's World Headquarters. Though I cannot at this time give you plans for these items, with Mr. Ilitch's ownership of both the Tigers and the Red Wings, I believe we may ultimately see a Sports Museum in Detroit. Your brother's items will certainly be a valuable addition to this effort.
If, in the future, you have any further questions, please feel free to contact me directly. The Ilitch organization certainly appreciates inclusion of these items in our Archives.

Very truly yours,

DETROIT TIGERS, INC.
Gerald M. Pasternak
Chief Financial Officer

Note:
Thanks to the Detroit Tigers Baseball Club and especially to Alice Sloane for tracking down the 1934 uniform.

153

V. EPILOGUE

In July '91, Chuck Hildebrand wrote in the Palo Alto Times Tribune:

"With Passing of Owen, the Santa Clara Valley Lost its Lefty O'Doul

The obituaries, predictably, focused on Marv Owen's involvement in one of the more infamous tableaus of baseball history. They also recited his numerical legacy: 9 solid major league seasons, World Series appearances in 1934 and 1935 with a ring to show for the latter, his presence in a Detroit Tigers infield that produced runs to an extent unparalled before or since.

Those were obituaries for this generation's consumption, and they were written with only a cursory glance through the shroud of time. Owen — who died last Saturday at a Mountain View nursing home at the age of 85 — represented something more, something more easily felt than expressed, to another generation in another Santa Clara Valley, in which the closest thing to toxic waste was a pile of rotting prunes.

THE VALLEY IN WHICH Marv Owen grew up was one of the most fertile fruit-growing regions in the world. San Jose had perhaps 50,000 people when Owen left Santa Clara University in 1930 to sign with the Seattle Indians of the Pacific Coast League. It was isolated even from the outlying villages from which it now is indistinguishable. It was far enough from the mainstream to make the nation's athletic icons more abstract than real. So it worshiped its tangible icons, the guys who came out of the prune orchards and the canneries, who made it all the way from the dusty environs of Sodality Park to the

major leagues. Even a San Francisco Seal was an individual to be admired. A major leaguer was a deity, a tie to a world otherwise inaccessible.

San Francisco's icon of another day was Lefty O'Doul, whose death in 1969 was mourned as a loss of the personification of what that city once represented. The Santa Clara Valley — the Santa Clara Valley that no longer exists — last Saturday lost its Lefty O'Doul.

Owen was not the first major leaguer to emerge from the valley. The infamous Hal Chase was born in Los Gatos. Mark Koenig, a Yankee infielder in the 1920s and 1930s, grew up in the valley although he was born in San Francisco. Frank Chance of Tinker-to-Evers-to-Chance fame often played in the area, having grown up in what now is Fremont. But Owen was the first major leaguer to be born in the valley, to learn the game there and to stay there until he left to the PCL. He was perhaps the Santa Clara Valley's most admired sports figure up to that time, and for some time afterward.

He was admired in Detroit, and was successful in business there during his career. But he came home after his playing career was over, and he stayed. Owen was the first manager of the San Jose team in the California League after the city was given a franchise in 1947, and his personal popularity was one reason it thrived. He lent his name and his time to the various youth programs that were coming into existence at that time. It there was a fund-raiser to be done or a judgment to be made concerning baseball in the valley, Owen invariably was asked. He almost never said no.

UNTIL FOUR OR FIVE years ago, Owen was as

much a fixture in the SCU athletic offices as the secretaries. His involvement with the baseball program was more than peripheral, even as he approached his 80s, and his counsel remained coveted. He was completely without pretense. If you weren't introduced to him as such, you'd never know he once was a major league baseball star.

Above all, he represented class. A few years ago, while doing a story on him, I asked him if he would be willing to commit to print his version of the Joe Medwick incident during the 1934 World Series. He'd never told his side, at least not completely.
'I'd like to', he said then! 'I've read versions of what happened and then asked myself, was I really there, because that wasn't what I remember. But Joe (Medwick) is dead. I'd like people to hear my side, but I would never say anything about what happened if the other guy involved isn't there to read it.'

It doesn't matter now what happened that day in 1934. It matters, at least to those who remember him, that Marv Owen was here."

October 21,1989 when Marv was asked by Dave Anderson of the New York Times "what he's most proud of in his long life, Marv didn't mention any of his baseball accomplishments. Instead he glanced at his son. 'Him,' he said. 'He's a good kid.'"

Marv, Skip and Jim

Marvin Owen

MARV OWEN   Major League Career

Year	Team	G	AB	R	H	RBI	BB	AVG	SO	FA
1931	Det-A	105	377	35	84	39	29	223	38	.937
1933	Det-A	138	550	77	144	65	44	262	56	.944
1934	Det-A*	154	565	79	179	96	59	317	37	.956
1935	Det-A*	134	483	52	127	71	43	263	37	.958
1936	Det-A	154	583	72	172	105	53	295	41	.952
1937	Det-A	107	396	48	114	45	41	288	24	.970
1938	Chi-A	141	577	84	162	55	45	281	31	.948
1939	Chi-A	58	194	22	46	15	16	237	15	.953
1940	Bos-A	20	57	4	12	6	8	211	4	.962
TOTAL 9 yrs		1011	3782	473	1040	497	338	275	283	.953

*World Series

Owen's big league career was distinguished by three unusual feats. He equalled a major league record by hitting four doubles in a game, April 23, 1939, and he made two unassisted double plays as a third baseman in successive games, April 28 and 29, 1934. He was a member of the 1934 Detroit Tigers infield holding the record for the most RBI's (462).

His total of 31 homeruns ranks him 1,400 out of 5,863 batters who have hit home runs.

BIBLIOGRAPHY

Books

- Berkow, Ira, Hank Greenberg, The Story of My Life, Times-Books, a division of Random House Inc., 1989

- Carter, Craig, and Sloan, Dave, The Sporting News, Baseball Guide, 1993 edition, The Sporting News Publishing Co., St. Louis, MO, 1993

- Carter, Craig, The Sporting News Complete Baseball Record Book, 1993 edition, The Sporting News Publishing Co., St. Louis, MO 1992

- Cohen, Richard M., Neff, David,, The World Series, Macmillan Co., 1986

- Dobbins, Dick, Twichell, Jon, Nuggets on the Diamond, Woodford Press, 1994

- Evers, John J., and Fullerton, Hugh S., Touching Second, Reilly & Britton Co., Chicago, 1910

- Honig, Donald, Baseball in the '30s, Crown Publisher's Inc., N.Y., 1989

- Kirkland, Bill, Eddie Neville of the Durham Bulls, McFarland and Co., 1993

- McConnell, Bob and Vincent, David W., Editors The Home Run Encyclopedia, Macmillan, 1996

- O'Neal, Bill, The Pacific Coast League, 1903-1988, Eakin Press, 1990

- Reichler, Joseph L., revised by Samelson, Ken, The Great All-Time Baseball Record Book, Macmillan, N.Y., 1993

- Thorn, John and Palmer, Pete, Gershman, Michael, Total Baseball, Harper Collins, 1993

Newspapers

- Detroit Free Press
- New York Times
- The Detroit News (Detroit Times)
- The Oregonian (Portland)
- The San Jose Mercury News
- The Santa Cruz County Sentinel
- The Sporting News

Journals and Reviews

- Kabacinski, Ronald, and Smith, James A., Baseball Quarterly Reviews, "Triple Plays at Navin Field, Briggs Stadium, Tiger Stadium," Vol. 7, No. 1, 1992

- Smith, James A. and Krabbenhoft, Herman, Baseball Research Journal, "Fenway Park Triple Plays," Vol. 8, No. 2, 1994

- Smith, Rick, Baseball Research Journal (SABR) article "Clutch Hitting or Good Fortune," #22, 1993

Agencies and/or Organizations

- Amateur Foundation, Los Angeles
- Bettmann Archive, New York
- Detroit Tiger Organization, MI
- Holy Name Society, Laurel Springs, New Jersey
- La Pere Collectibles, MI
- National Baseball Library and Archive, Cooperstown, NY
- Ripley Entertainment, Inc., Orlando, Florida
- University of Santa Clara, CA

Video-tape

- Padon, Dwayne and Hayworth, Ray, Gehringer/Greenberg Day, 1983

INDEX